D0024672

THE
DEVIL'S
ADVOCATES

THE DEVIL'S ADVOCATES

Decadence in Modern Literature

THOMAS REED WHISSEN

Contributions to the Study of World Literature, Number 33

GREENWOOD PRESS

New York
Westport, Connecticut
London

Library of Congress Cataloging-in-Publication Data

Whissen, Thomas R.
  The Devil's advocates : decadence in modern literature / Thomas
Reed Whissen.
    p. cm. — (Contributions to the study of world literature.
ISSN 0738-9345 ; no. 33)
  Includes index.
  Bibliography: p.
  ISBN 0-313-26483-X (lib. bdg. : alk. paper)
  1. Literature, Modern—19th century—History and criticism.
2. Literature, Modern—20th century—History and criticism.
3. Decadence in literature. I. Title. II. Series.
PN761.W45 1989
809'.91—dc19   89-2108

British Library Cataloguing in Publication Data is available.

Copyright © 1989 by Thomas Reed Whissen

All rights reserved. No portion of this book may be
reproduced, by any process or technique, without the
express written consent of the publisher.

Library of Congress Catalog Card Number: 89-2108
ISBN: 0-313-26483-X
ISSN: 0738-9345

First published in 1989

Greenwood Press, Inc.
88 Post Road West, Westport, Connecticut 06881

Printed in the United States of America

The paper used in this book complies with the
Permanent Paper Standard issued by the National
Information Standards Organization (Z39.48-1984).

10 9 8 7 6 5 4 3 2 1

HUGH STEPHENS LIBRARY
STEPHENS COLLEGE
COLUMBIA, MISSOURI

PN
761
.W45
1989

To Anni

for love, for life, forever

197501

NOOR STEPHENS LIBRARY
STEPHENS COLLEGE
COLUMBIA, MISSOURI

No one who wholeheartedly shares in a given sensibility can analyze it; he can only, whatever his intentions, exhibit it. To name a sensibility, to draw its contours and to recount its history, requires a deep sympathy modified by revulsion.

Susan Sontag, "Notes on 'Camp'"

Contents

Preface

Decadence is a term we all use quite freely and with a fairly good idea of what we mean by it. But even when we know what *we* mean, we are not always sure we know what *it* means. Unfortunately, most attempts to pin it down invariably end in frustration.

Rigorous scholarly minds have wrestled with the term with only mixed success. Those who stay within the narrow confines of late nineteenth-century French and English literature have reached a somewhat uneasy compromise on the term's usefulness in describing a significant literary affectation of that period, but the use of the term in any wider context continues to be hotly debated. In the preface to *Aesthetes and Decadents of the 1890s,* Karl Beckson says that the attempt to state precisely what decadence means "has led numerous literary historians to dash themselves on the semantic rocks" (vii). The frustration of it has even tempted some scholars to abandon the attempt. In fact, in *Decadence: The Strange Life of an Epithet,* Richard Gilman argues almost too convincingly in favor of banishing "this injured and vacant word from history." Otherwise, he says, it "will go on recommending itself to the shallow, the thoughtless and imitative, the academically frozen: monkey-minds" (180).

Who can resist a challenge like that? Gilman is right, of course, in lamenting the fact that decadence is an overused and overworked word and in fearing that one more attempt to define it will only add to the confusion surrounding it and contribute to its uselessness. However, there are certain threads running through modern literature that can be appreciated only if they can be seen as interwoven parts of the fabric known as decadence.

In *Decadence: A Philosophical Inquiry,* a thorough and provocative (if somewhat prejudiced) analysis of the subject, philosopher C.E.M. Joad says that he does not think there is any word "whose meaning is vaguer and more difficult to define than the word 'decadence' [nor one] which is used in a greater variety of senses" (55). This multiplicity of usage is not only a result of the word's vagueness, he argues, but also a contributor to it. Robert Adams, in *Decadent Societies,* agrees that the word's offenses are "many and grievous," but feels that the word is not beyond rehabilitation (2).

Failure to find a common definition for so popular a term is no reason to throw out a word that has such beguiling connotations and for which there is no really acceptable substitute. And why, anyway, must we all agree on what a word means before we feel free to use it? After all, many of the most indispensable words in the language are fraught with ambiguity and contradiction. Lively disagreement about their meaning only increases their vitality.

Because decadence is such a controversial term, any definition that pleases some is bound to offend others. Although I do not presume to settle the matter, I do think that there is common ground on which students of decadence can meet and possibly agree. Therefore, rather than try to suggest a dictionary definition of this protean term, I have chosen to offer a list of what I have found to be the principal elements of decadence, elements derived primarily from a close reading of Joris-Karl Huysmans' *Against Nature (À Rebours).* Published in Paris in 1884, this fictional biography of the quintessential decadent, Duc Jean Floressas des Esseintes, has since become the acknowledged handbook of decadence, influencing (some would say contaminating) everyone it touched when it first appeared and altering the course of literature ever since. Sensitive, sophisticated, cynical, snobbish, and vain, Des Esseintes is a figure whose personality had already been anticipated in the neurotic narrator of Dostoyevsky's *Notes from Underground* and which was destined to reappear in one form or another from Sherlock Holmes and Dorian Gray to Elliott Templeton in *The Razor's Edge* and Guy Huber in *Social Disease.* Few of Des Esseintes's fictional descendants have lived a life of such dedicated decadence as his, but more than a few have come close.

Although there is rarely anything in twentieth-century literature approaching the intensity of the decadent literature of the late nineteenth century, there are nevertheless unmistakable traces of the influence of that movement—certainly of the presence of decadent elements, however they got there—in the works of a surprising number of twentieth-century writers both in Europe and the United States. The fires may have cooled, but they have not gone out. For this reason, decadence continues to attract the attention of critics who see it, according to Beckson, as "not only an absorbing chapter in literary history and taste, but also [as] a significant prelude to and major influence on contemporary literature." Beckson describes the relationship between the literature of the decadent period and that of modern times as a "similar quest for new experience and for new forms of expression in a world bereft of unassailable truths" (vii).

The danger in tracking a concept like decadence is the risk of forcing the issue, of begging the question: Which comes first, the definition or the representation? That is why I stay fairly close to the letter of *Against Nature,* although at times I feel justified in making additional claims for the spirit of the work. In spite of its reputation for unrelieved perversity, the book is surprisingly moral and impressively erudite. Fully half of it is devoted to several well-informed treatises on art, literature, and music, not to mention philosophy and religion. And while the opinions of its central character, Des Esseintes, may betray an unrepentant bias, it is the educated bias of an astute critic. Des Esseintes readily admits that his preference in literature is for books that match his own thinking, a good example right there of decadent egoism.

While most of the scholarship that has gathered around this intriguing topic is well intentioned, too much of it has been either needlessly polemical or embarrassingly defensive. One gets the feeling that some scholars think the choice is between chewing the carpet or biting one's nails. Since the word decadence continues to have what Joad calls a "smell" to it, some scholars fear guilt by association. Joad himself worries about the difficulty of scholarly objectivity when one is dealing with such a controversial topic. "It is exceedingly difficult to cite any examples of decadence in literature which would be generally accepted as such," he says, and because of this, one finds oneself "fatally entangled in the relativities and subjectivities of one's own personal taste or of the taste of the times to which one belongs" (64).

Robert Adams maintains that "the person who chooses decadence as a topic is not necessarily contaminated by it, is not to be supposed decadent himself" (6). Be that as it may, I prefer to think that you need to have more than an objective knowledge of anything you get involved in if you do not want your treatment of it to end up lifeless and unconvincing. It would be very difficult, I should think, to write convincingly about decadence if there were no trace of passion in your approach, be it fascination or loathing.

I think I share enough of the decadent temper to be able, like a geiger counter or a dog sniffing for drugs, to detect the presence of decadent elements wherever they appear in modern literature. This affinity with the decadent temper has given me the confidence to make claims, some of them quite bold, about works of literature not ordinarily thought of as having any connection with decadence. I have no doubt that I shall stand accused of stretching the point, of finding decadence wherever I choose to find it or of seeing it when it is not really there. All I can say in response is that the decadent aesthetic has had such a pervasive influence on the modern mind that it would be remarkable if it did not have a discernible effect on modern literature as part of the rhetoric of fiction. This does not make modern literature predominantly decadent by any means, any more than it places in the decadent mainstream those authors who exhibit elements of decadence in their works. What I do contend is that traces of the influence of the decadent movement are to be found throughout modern literature and that it is time we took a look at them to see what they can tell us about what we read and who we are. If, along the way, the study itself turns decadent, I offer no apologies. After all, what self-respecting author could present to the public a book about decadence unless that book itself had something of the "smell" about it?

Some of the things I like about decadence are the impertinence of its wit, the affectations of its style, the archness of its posturing, the thumbing of its elegant nose. I think it's all great fun as long as you don't take it—or at least yourself—too seriously. But I am also keenly aware of the disturbing side of decadence, the dark side that is selfish, elitist, uncharitable, reactionary, and vain, a side all too easily obsessed with those humorless preoccupations that give it its reputation for unwholesomeness.

To those who see only its dark side and are convinced that it is not only a sign of cultural deterioration but a contributor to it, decadence is something to be abhorred. They see no reason to accept, much less celebrate, the decline of civilization. However, to those who find the concept useful both as a critical term and as a cultural attitude, decadence is no more than a mirror of reality. To them, decadence looks the devil in the eye—and winks. If civilization is dying, they say, decadents will see to it that it goes out in style.

It is easier, I think, to *sense* the meaning of decadence if you can personify it. I see a decadent as something of a Beau Brummell, impeccably dressed, with worldly good looks, a sardonic smile, and a devastating wit; a charming skeptic, fighting vainly the old ennui, adrift in a world he finds increasingly unmannered and vulgar, a world devoted to a spiteful egalitarianism, torn by petty rivalries, awash in nasty hypocrisies: in short, a world in which he can survive only if he keeps his distance.

The problem is that a jaundiced view of the world gives one *carte blanche* to indulge in whatever one likes, to get away with whatever one can while there is still world enough and time. And no one would argue that this relaxed attitude is not present in the decadent temper. But to see decadence as indiscriminate intemperance is to miss the point. Decadents are not drunks or dopers or sex fiends or gluttons. They are more apt to be hedonists of the spirit rather than the flesh. In fact, all too often their spirit continues to be willing long after their flesh has grown weak.

The decadent is more a dandy than a Bohemian. As art historian Arnold Hauser describes him, "he is the bourgeois intellectual taken out of his proper class into a higher one, while the Bohemian is the artist who has sunk down to the proletariat. The fastidious elegance and extravagance of the dandy," he says, "fulfills the same function as the depravity and dissipation of the bohemians" (*Social,* 904).

Like Baudelaire's image of the dandy, he is "the living indictment of a standardizing democracy," uniting within himself "all the gentlemanly virtues that are still possible today; he is a match for every situation and is never astonished at anything; he never becomes vulgar and always preserves the cool smile of the stoic." He is "the last revelation of heroism in an age of decadence, a sunset, a last radiant beam of human pride" (904).

Decadence, then, is simply another way of looking at the world, and like any other *Weltanschauung,* it is, at bottom, a defense against dread. To grant decadence this philosophical status is to accord it the legitimacy it deserves. In a society desperate to increase the length but not the quality of life, decadence is a mockery of such vanity. In a world hasty to accept the wrong answers but reluctant to ask the right questions, decadence insists on raising those questions: Why are we here? Why do we bother? How do we face the unknown—or the known, for that matter? The dread is there in all of us, and as a way of defending ourselves against it, we search desperately for explanations, or at least consolations. Decadence can offer both, and perhaps this is why Beckson believes that "for most modern critics, the term . . . does not carry pejorative connotations" (vii). It may be an attitude, but like all attitudes, it is also something of an answer.

Throughout this study I use the term *decadence* to identify certain elements which, while not new to literature in general, have become increasingly apparent in western literature since the decadent movement of the late nineteenth century. Because I have restricted this study to the literatures of no more than a half dozen western countries, I do not claim to have exhausted the possibilities of finding decadence in unfamiliar or unexpected places. My method throughout this study is to dwell at length on a relatively short list of works, some because they are generally accepted as works that contain elements of decadence, others because I wish to use them to demonstrate the continuing influence of the decadent tradition. This list includes *Against Nature* by J.-K. Huysmans, *The Picture of Dorian Gray* by Oscar Wilde, *The Spoils of Poynton* by Henry James, *The Immoralist* by André Gide, *Death in Venice* by Thomas Mann, *Seven Gothic Tales* by Isak Dinesen, *Perfume* by Patrick Süskind, and *Social Disease* by Paul Rudnick. These works are sufficient, I think, to set the stage because they contain examples of most of the elements I have isolated. In each chapter, therefore, I return to these works for examples of the particular element of decadence under discussion.

With the exception of *Seven Gothic Tales,* published in 1934, and *Perfume* and *Social Disease,* both published in 1986, these works first appeared at or near the time that decadence was becoming a major concept and an important influence in modern western literature. As for the rest of modern literature, I make use of as much of it as I think fits, referring mostly to familiar names and works, but pausing here and there to acknowledge some less familiar ones who have either been critically neglected or who have yet to make their mark. Among them there are, I am sure, a few who deserve to be relegated to oblivion. I refer to them in order to make a point, not to rescue a reputation.

Some readers are bound to object to some of the authors and titles I dare to associate with decadence while others are likely to regret the absence of names they would like to see added to the list. Since I am constantly revising my own list as I reappraise familiar voices and discover new ones, I can only beg the indulgence of readers on both sides and urge them to share their lists—and their laments—with me.

Introduction

Although elements of decadence can be found in literary works of all periods, decadence is essentially a modern movement. It has its roots in the romantic movement of the early nineteenth century, and it flowered in the last two decades of that century; but it did not, as some say, wither and die in the twentieth. On the contrary, precisely because it expresses a malaise that commonly pervades both life and art at the end of a century, it would be remarkable if decadence were not even more pervasive in life and art at the end of a millennium.

If decadence seems less obvious now than it did a century ago, the reason is simply that many of the elements of decadence, once rare enough to stand out, are now such a part of our reality that we simply fail to see them as decadent. Or if we do see them, we may misinterpret them, for decadence is relative to the times and will always resist identification with what is in the mainstream. It is time, then, to refocus our vision and look at modern literature—and life—from the peculiar perspective of decadence.

Until the late nineteenth century, it was generally held that literature was supposed to be positive, that regardless of its content, its message ought to be uplifting. Vice appeared only to highlight virtue, and unwholesome behavior, however lovingly depicted, was invariably punished. Literature was meant to be instructive and exemplary, a record of the progress of mankind towards perfection. This is not to say that this was the way literature was always written—or received. But by a sort of silent consensus, this was its accepted purpose, and those who thought otherwise either held their tongues or went underground.

In any age it is not unusual to find an underground literature that runs counter to the mainstream literature of that age. *Fanny Hill* is only the most famous example of the subculture available to the neoclassicists of the eighteenth century. The graveyard poets, though not disreputable, were certainly not entirely respectable: all that morbidity and melancholy, that languishing over tombstones and baying at gibbous moons.

Decadence might have taken root in romanticism, but its seeds were sewn by the charlatans and macaronies of the preceding age. First there was Macpherson, the Scottish forger who "translated" from Gaelic into English several notorious but highly acclaimed epic poems presumably written by a third-century bardic hero by the name of Ossian, poems which Macpherson claimed he had found in a cave. Then came Thomas Chatterton, that "marvellous boy" and patron saint of the romantics, a brilliant fraud who died by his own hand at seventeen, a "martyr to poetry," after faking a slew of poems "bye makeing themme looke lyke thys" and attributing them to a nonexistent fifteenth-century monk, poet, and antiquarian named Thomas Rowley.

What a figure Macpherson and Chatterton would have cut a century and a half later when their forgeries would have been venerated as inspired chicanery worthy of an age practiced in deceit. In his biography of Oscar Wilde, Richard Ellmann says that Wilde was fascinated with Chatterton because of Chatterton's "criminal propensities" (284). Wilde, he says, found an analogue to his own way of life in this young man who "used his genius to forge Jacobean plays." Ellmann describes Chatterton as a self-destructive poet with whom Wilde could share "Hamlet's doubt and Satan's pride," and says that Wilde had a sense of forging a life as Chatterton had done, sensing that one day he might "be his own victim, a sacrifice to himself" (285). It turned out, alas, to be a self-fulfilling prophecy.

Although in its shattered idealism and its melancholy sense of alienation decadence is the pale child of romanticism, it is indebted to the eighteenth century for two powerful influences, one bright, one dark. On the bright side of the legacy is the urbanity of the neoclassical "man of the world," someone like Lord Chesterfield, a gentleman of wise and witty counsel, a realist, someone in whom charity and cynicism were mixed in equal measure. Satire, the comedy of manners, a preference for style over content, artificiality: these were things the decadents returned to and made their own. And certainly it is not too great a leap from the wigged and buckled fops of the Pump Room to the gilded lilies of a mauve salon.

On the dark side of the legacy is the shadow of the Marquis de Sade, the celebrated erotomaniac who, by giving deviancy his good name, gave decadence a bad one. The truth is that de Sade was too humorless to be a decadent. For a Frenchman, he went about his "sadism" with Teutonic diligence. Moreover, his brand of cruelty was simply too painful, too physical for the decadents of a century later, whose painful pleasures tended to be more cerebral. But his influence is undeniably there, particularly in fostering a taste for the bizarre and in presenting a rationale for moral rebellion. His understanding of abnormal psychology suited the mood of the late Victorians and prepared them for the liberating influence of Sigmund Freud. While they avoided de Sade's excesses, they admired him for the courage of his perversions.

By the end of the nineteenth century decadence was an idea whose time had come. It had already overtaken French literature where, along with its bedfellow symbolism, it had revolutioned French letters—and scandalized (if that's ever truly possible) French society. Imported into England, however, decadence never did become anything more than naughty. When it surfaced, it almost immediately sought acceptance by acquiring a patina of respectability. This it did by tempering its tone to become more amusing than abrasive, more surprising than shocking.

Set against drab, grim, polluted London of what Robert Adams calls the "gray" nineties, the outlandish fashions and eccentric affectations of Oscar Wilde and his crowd seem more sad than silly. The world they saw, the world they had unwillingly inherited, had been made unbelievably ugly, in a relatively short time, by all the horrors accompanying a rapidly expanding industrial society, especially one that lacked the experience to know how to handle pollution and sanitation, poor working conditions, and overcrowded cities.

Looking about them at what must have seemed a hopeless situation—a social worker's nightmare—the sensitive artists of the times rebelled in the only way they knew how, the only way left—inwardly. They saw no possibility whatsoever of reforming society, and so they set about distancing themselves from it. They fancied themselves "aesthetes," choosing "art for art's sake" as their credo. Since nothing artistic seemed to have any effect whatsoever on a society determined to glorify bad taste, these aesthetes could only conclude that "all art is useless" and take whatever satisfaction they could in producing works that existed only for their own sake. In fact, they soon came to elevate literary criticism to the position of the highest art form, maintaining that if art is a notch above reality, criticism is a notch above art.

"The first duty in life is to be as artificial as possible," Oscar Wilde announced. Artificial, he said, not shocking or disgraceful or obnoxious. "What the second duty is no one has yet discovered," he added. People found this remark amusing and inoffensive, and they still do. It has about it the urbanity of a Cole Porter lyric, not the vulgarity of a Lenny Bruce monologue. But beneath Wilde's pronouncement there lurks a serious question: How do you behave in a world that is itself artificial?

The behavior that Wilde and others like him affected as an answer to this question was described as decadent by both admirers and detractors. His detractors associated the term with all that was morally offensive in *fin-de-siècle* France; his admirers preferred to associate it with the high-spirited, nose-tweaking insouciance of *la belle époque.* But when Wilde's life ended in disgrace, the term took on more sinister connotations and has suffered a very dubious reputation ever since. This is why it is easy to dismiss decadence as an aberration peculiar to a short-lived literary period and overlook the fact that it was the expression of a temper that has influenced much of modern literature in the twentieth century right down to the present time.

One problem a student of decadence in literature has is trying to figure out whether a work is itself decadent or whether it simply deals with decadent themes. In *Decadent Style,* John Reed makes a useful distinction between "decadent novels" and "novels of decadence." Huysmans' *Against Nature* he calls a decadent novel whereas Wilde's *The Picture of Dorian Gray* he calls a novel of decadence. The fact is that few works are exclusively decadent, and few of those that are have lasted. *Against Nature* is well known among decadent scholars, but it is too esoteric for most tastes, and the five slender novels of Ronald Firbank are now mostly neglected by all but a few devoted fans. The same can be said of such relatively obscure titles as Aubrey Beardsley's *Under the Hill* or Cyril Connolly's *The Unquiet Grave.* Even Max Beerbohm, sometimes the scapegrace, sometimes the scourge of the decadents, might find himself ironically consigned to share their oblivion if only because *Zuleika Dobson,* a delightful parody of decadence, shares with such parodies as Robert Hichens's *The Green Carnation* and G.S. Street's *The Autobiography of a Boy* the sad fate of no longer having an audience that can appreciate the parody.

After the second world war, Truman Capote was our reigning decadent writer for several decades, but now it looks as if he will be remembered more for *In Cold Blood* than for *Other Voices, Other Rooms* or *The Grass Harp.* And Gore Vidal is likely to be remembered more for *Lincoln* than for *Myra Breckenridge,* even though *Myra Breckenridge* is much more original—and a lot more entertaining. A more recent addition to the list of decadent novels is Paul Rudnick's *Social Disease,* a delightful work, fully as outrageous and funny as Firbank's fluff and probably just as doomed.

Of interest also to students of the decadent influence in modern literature are the novels of Ian McEwan, Michael Chabon, and Patrick Süskind. McEwan is an English writer whose most decadent work, *The Comfort of Strangers,* is a sinister story of perversity and obsession set in contemporary Venice and reminiscent of the menacing atmosphere of *The Aspern Papers* and *Death in Venice.* Michael Chabon is an American writer whose first novel, *The Mysteries of Pittsburgh,* exhibits traces of the decadent influence in the behavior of its offbeat characters and in the atmosphere it evokes. For a first novel, it is stylistically mature, emotionally challenging, and irresistibly believable even when it tests the limits of credibility. Patrick Süskind is a German writer who, in his remarkable first novel, *Perfume,* creates an eighteenth-century monster of a protagonist who becomes almost a parody of most of the major elements of decadence.

Our concern here, however, is primarily with mainstream literature in which elements of decadence appear either as part of a writer's attitude (e.g., Tom Wolfe's merry despair) or as rhetorical devices (e.g., the presence of a decadent character like Anthony Blanche in *Brideshead Revisited*). In works such as Thomas Mann's *Death in Venice* and André Gide's *The Immoralist,* decadence is presented in the context of moral commentary. Even so, the line between decadent books and books about decadence is frequently finer than Reed would have it. The same fascination with decadence that attracts a writer to portray it can sometimes tempt the writer to purvey it as well. Like the dancer and the dance, it is not always possible to separate decadent style from decadent theme.

Each chapter of this study is devoted to the analysis and illustration of one of the elements common to decadence as it makes its presence known in representative works of modern literature. My purpose is to examine what these works have in common and to analyze how those common ingredients operate to accommodate a specific literary purpose.

Decadence shares with existentialism a stubborn resistance to textbook definition. Just as any attempt at a precise definition of existentialism would destroy existentialism's very meaning, so would a precise definition of decadence drain the vitality from that term. We murder not only to dissect, it seems, but also to define. Rather than add to the confusion surrounding the meaning of decadence, I would prefer to think of my extended definition as more of an explanation of how decadence has made itself felt in modern literature and why it continues to wield an influence. This approach respects the integrity of the concept by presenting it less as a transient literary anomaly and more as a viable way of coming to terms with a baffling world. The result should be a clearer picture of the function of decadence not only in modern literature but in modern life.

In a refreshingly unmuddled essay, "Late Victorian Decadence," Russell Goldfarb argues that the controversy over conflicting and confusing definitions of decadence is pointless for two basic reasons. First, he points out quite convincingly that critics from Arthur Symons to C.E.M. Joad have given us a compositive understanding of what decadence, or at least late Victorian decadence, is and says that "until this understanding of decadence is shown to be inadequate, it hardly seems necessary to write toward a new definition" (373). Second, he gives examples to prove that authors within the decadent movement "concerned themselves with exploiting popular ideas about whatever single quality of decadence best suited their purposes." To Max Beerbohm, he says, "decadence was artifice; to Robert Hichens, it was unconventional and exhibitionist behavior; to John Davidson and Jocelyn Quilp, it was immorality, to G.S. Street, the lust for unusual experience. After 1900," he adds, "most of the people who wrote about decadence defined the term for use as a standard of literary criticism. They put together several attributes common to decadent literature and formed a definition" (371). This is a fair description of what I try to do in this book.

Before we begin to consider what decadence is, it would be wise to take a look at what it is not. Perhaps because alliteration is so tempting, decadence has come to be associated with a long list of words beginning with the letter "D": decay, decline, deterioration, depravity, debauchery, disintegration, degeneration, dissipation—the list goes on. Because just about anything bad you care to say about decadence is apt to ring true, words like these have taken on the power of synonyms. While it is clear that decadence appears at a time when a civilization seems doomed and corruption rampant, this is merely the *Zeitgeist* in which decadence flourishes, not the essence of decadence itself.

In the introduction to her bibliography of the decadent period, Linda Dowling comments on the persistence of the *fin-de-siècle* myth and on the way it has affected the modern imagination, especially at the end of a century that is also the end of a millennium. Some common characteristics she points to are the fascination with youth and personality, the tendency of a generation to identify itself through a characteristic style, and the inclination to assign descriptive labels to decades. She mentions "aesthetic eighties" and "naughty nineties," but in this century, while the "roaring twenties" may be our only enduring label, we still refer to decades as though they were whole generations, applying such labels as "silent" to the fifties and the "me decade" to the seventies and knowing exactly what we mean by a "sixties mentality" or a "woman of the eighties." She finds the source for this pursuit of the faddish in late nineteenth-century avant-gardism, an intense desire not merely to keep up but to stay ahead (x).

Dowling also finds as part of the myth of the *fin de siècle* what she calls "the presentation of the self as performance" coupled with a "conviction of cultural decay" (x), elements that have been associated historically with decadent periods in which a cult of the self emerges and there is a collective shrugging of the shoulders and a growing mood of cheerful hopelessness. She goes on to say that while some writers will deride the myth as a "pernicious and ineradicable caricature of the period," it is inevitable that others "will continue to invoke it and its major emphases, especially as the twentieth-century *fin de siècle* approaches" (x). We shall see how this myth can lead those who invoke it into unexpected alliances with forces that are clever at exploiting its curious mixture of narcissism, masochism, and nihilism.

Even though decadents may accept the decline of civilization as inevitable and therefore unstoppable, they do not rejoice at its passing. They merely feel powerless to resist it and are morbidly amused by those who, in the name of arresting the decline, unwittingly accelerate it. Unlike revolutionaries, decadents do not rebel, but they may at times feel tempted to surrender, and not just to the melancholy reality of decay but even to the lassitude that hastens it. In *The Magic Mountain,* Thomas Mann allegorizes this tendency in the character of Hans Castorp, a tubercular young man, "half in love with easeful death" as Keats once described himself in similar circumstances, who surrenders to his disease as he might to a voluptuous but tainted seductress.

Unfortunately, decadence is often mistakenly associated with ugliness and filth and sleaze. Nothing could be further from the truth. In fact, it is precisely from the noisome that decadents recoil. Their taste is for the more agreeable vices such as pride with maybe just a touch of sloth and a tad of envy thrown in, victimless sins, but sins with a hint of self-destruction about them; for decadents are obsessively self-conscious, loving themselves one moment, hating themselves the next. It is no wonder, then, that elements of decadence are present in so much contemporary literature. If we do not always spot them at first glance, it may be that they are too close to see or simply that they are too close for comfort.

Another popular misconception about decadence is that it can be used to describe the life of anyone who runs afoul of the law or commits a socially offensive act. There are many people who enjoy boasting of their so-called decadent behavior and telling stories on themselves about how wicked and evil they are, but their wickedness is usually dreary and their evil banal. Eventually they appear on television talk-shows where they parade their sins in a parody of confession and contrition, or else they speciously justify them in the name of some recently dreamed-up "right" to something or other. From drug pushers to rapists, from pornographers to serial murderers, from wife beaters to child molesters, they betray an astonishing lack of honest remorse as they blame society for all their fun. This is not decadence; this is just the rotten side of human nature.

Decadence is Boccaccio's elegant ladies and gentlemen gathered on a hillside, diverting themselves with amusing stories while the plague ravages Florence down below. Decadence is Henry James's Hyacinth Robinson in *The Princess Casamassima,* reclining on a magenta divan in Venice, smoking cigarettes and worrying about the poor. Decadence is what happens when artistic optimism confronts historical pessimism. Holbrook Jackson, in his classic book on the nineties, says of that period:

It was an era of hope and action. People thought anything might happen; and, for the young, any happening sufficiently new was good. Little of the older sentimentalism survived among the modernists; those who were of the period desired to be in the movement, and not mere spectators. It was a time of experiment. Dissatisfied with the long ages of convention and action which arose out of the precedent, many set about testing life for themselves. The new man wished to be himself, the new woman threatened to live her own life. . . . Never indeed, was there a time when the young were so young or the old so old (30).

Decadent minor poets sprang up in the most unexpected places. The staidest of nonconformist circles begot strange, pale youths with abundant hair, whose abandoned thoughts expressed themselves in "purple patches" of prose, and whose sole aim in life was to live "passionately" in a succession of "scarlet moments." Life-tasting was the fashion, and the rising generation felt as though it were stepping out of the cages of convention and custom into a freedom full of tremendous possibilities (31).

The desire to live "passionately" in a succession of "scarlet moments" was the result of taking to heart Walter Pater's exhortation, in the conclusion to *Studies in the Renaissance,* to "burn with a gemlike flame," a passage he later deleted when he saw his disciples taking him all too literally. Although much of this spirit may seem to apply to the counterculture of the 1960s, the comparison is superficial and the differences enormous. While the "hippies" may have worn their hair long and indulged in "life-tasting," their mood was sullen and their manners coarse. And there was much hypocrisy present in what they thought and did. Deeply prejudiced, they railed against prejudice; unprecedentedly affluent, they derided affluence while accepting its subsidy. They used war to fight war and sophistry to outwit sophistry, and in matters of taste their instincts were unerringly wrong. In their avowed concern for the quality of life, they undermined whatever quality there was by rejecting anything that was not loud, demeaning, and obnoxious. And they did it deliberately, relentlessly, and all in the name of freedom. Such arrogant ignorance has rarely been equalled. It was Bohemianism without the redeeming quality of artistic talent.

All of this is anathema to the spirit of decadence because it lacks, in a word, class. The difference is perfectly illustrated in Somerset Maugham's brilliant short story, "The Outstation," in which a gentleman named Warburton clashes with a boor named Cooper. The time is just after the first world war, and the setting is a remote outpost deep in the jungles of Borneo where Warburton has lived alone for twenty years, sustained by a code of behavior totally incongruous with his surroundings. On his first evening there, Cooper arrives for dinner in casual clothes and is astonished to find Warburton wearing a starched shirt and dinner jacket. He asks Warburton if he dresses for dinner even when he is alone, to which Warburton replies: "Especially when I'm alone." It is a consummate decadent touch, reminiscent of Oscar Wilde who once told a friend, "If I were all alone marooned on a desert island and had my things with me, I should dress for dinner every evening" (Ellmann, 38).

Totally lacking in manners, Cooper disrupts not only Warburton's routine but the routine of the outstation as well. Because he cannot see the need for protocol in such a remote place, he is equally insensitive to the feelings of the natives who work for him. Eventually he is stabbed to death by a native with whom he has dealt unjustly, and Warburton is free to continue his life as it was, a life that can only be endured with the support of unexamined ritual, what Thomas Mann in *Death in Venice* calls "the gracious bearing preserved in the stern, stark service of form" (446). Though this ritual may strike others as meaningless, its meaning lies in its very enactment. What Archibald MacLeish said about poetry can also be said about ritual: it should not *mean* but *be.* To the decadents, ritual for its own sake is the "ceremony of innocence" which is drowned out in the clamor of the vulgar spouting their designer dogmas.

Even though they may not worship there, decadents still honor the temple of tradition whereas the vulgar do it dishonor. Unfortunately, it is the vulgar who are full of "passionate intensity" while the decadents suffer from a debilitating failure of nerve; and where nerve is lacking there can be neither threat nor challenge. It is this very ineffectuality, therefore, this charming bravado that makes decadents so disarming—and ultimately so vulnerable. From Roderick Usher to Des Esseintes to J. Alfred Prufrock, lack of conviction has rendered the decadents morally impotent; and their counterparts are legion in modern literature. Gregor Samsa in Franz Kafka's "The Metamorphosis," a pathetic figure unable to withstand the oppression of job and family, is transformed into the insect that fits his self-image, and this metamorphosis symbolizes not only his failure of nerve but other characteristics of decadence such as alienation and masochism, irreverence and regret. Tibby in E.M. Forster's *Howards End* retreats to the dreaming spires of Oxford, Henry Pulling in Graham Greene's *Travels with My Aunt* would rather dawdle among his dahlias, Sebastian Flyte in Evelyn Waugh's *Brideshead Revisited* surrenders to a life of voluntary servitude.

Then there are those like Augustus von Schimmelmann in Isak Dinesen's "The Poet," or John Marcher in Henry James's "The Beast in the Jungle," men who spend their lives waiting for something to happen only to find out, when it is too late, that what has "happened" to them is precisely nothing. From more recent literature, there is the hero of Jay McInerney's *Bright Lights, Big City,* a young man who, according to the book jacket blurb, "can run but he can't hide," not to mention the outrageous *ménage à trois* of Paul Rudnick's *Social Disease,* a wacky trio of happy hedonists who have plenty of nerve in trivial matters and none whatsoever where it counts.

Decadents are in exile from the commonplace; they are emigrés in lotusland, detached from the world, apart from and, to their way of thinking, above the herd. They like to indulge in satire, most of it of the kind that scratches without scarring, just as they like to affect a cynicism that often masks a taste for camp. It is the wry cynicism of the Cole Porter lyric about the poor, enervated sophisticate who is bored stiff by champagne and cocaine but who manages to get at least some sort of kick from the chance for romance.

Decadence, as described thus far, may seem like an attitude hardly calculated to bother any but those who still believe that "you don't belong if you're just taking up space," or "if you're not solving the problem, you *are* the problem." However, there is still that dark and disturbing side of decadence, that side that can be summed up in one word: gullibility. And this gullibility takes many forms, from the relatively passive to the unmistakably pernicious. Since decadents, like Melville's Bartleby, "prefer not to" get involved, they may be secretly sympathetic to a cause but are loath to translate that sympathy into action. However, when this inclination to submit becomes religious or political,

the consequences can be alarming. In a world too overwhelming to be
grasped, a world in which systems of faith and governance vie for followers by
promising to bring order out of chaos, to simplify the complexities of modern
life, and to clear up once and for all the mystery of existence, the temptation
to give up the struggle and give in to a ready-made system is too great to be
easily resisted.

Decadence first flourished in the shadow of romanticism, and it has been
part of the dark history of the romantic movement to witness periodic waves
of surrender to institutions that could lift the burden of doubt from weary
shoulders and bring initiates to their knees in ecstatic submission. This has
been the history of many artists in the twentieth century, and it is decadence
that goes far to explain it. For it is so easy for the decadent temper to degenerate from harmless self-indulgence into insidious self-hypnosis.

Decadence thrives in an age that has outlived itself and suspects that the vandals are at the gates. The Edwardians, for example, lived as if the nineteenth
century had never ended, still performing the old rituals, following the old
rules, dancing to the old music. Underneath there was corruption and hypocrisy and a yearning for apocalypse. When the apocalypse came in the form of
the first world war, many thought it was the end of the world, but it was only
the end of one kind of world, and afterwards the "lost generation," in its efforts to drown out the voices of despair, found itself adding a new chapter to
the chronicle of decadence.

F. Scott Fitzgerald receiving Edith Wharton at his lodgings in a Paris
brothel is a decadent affectation. He wanted to shock her. That it didn't work,
that she was blissfully unaware of where she was—or, more likely, only pretended to be—may be the manifestation of a subtler level of decadence on her
part. Fitzgerald's own life of studied dissipation, not to mention the lives of
his lonely young heroes who torture themselves with winter dreams, who
cherish their broken hearts, who watch life from the sidelines: these are the
postures of decadence. And nowhere is this more evident than in *The Great
Gatsby,* a novel in which a sensitive young loner witnesses the splendid aloofness of the mysterious Jay Gatsby while Gatsby himself watches from a distance those diversions he arranges but does not take part in.

Expatriates of the sort found in Paris in the twenties are, by nature of their
self-imposed exile, borrowing from the decadent temper. Most of them lived
lives of dandified dissipation, gathering regularly in Bohemian bars and cafés
to discuss art and disparage the bourgeoisie. There they applauded Gertrude
Stein's compulsive refinement of the language and welcomed movements in
music and painting that would distance the faithful from the Philistines.
There is even a strain of dandyism in the early Hemingway of the period, not
only in his appearance but also in the famous prose style so carefully crafted to
look so utterly artless.

In the thirties and forties decadence is more visible in the world of entertainment where composers like Noel Coward and Cole Porter, with their clever concoctions of satire and sentimentality, catered to the rich, desperate to forget the crash, and to the poor, desperate to escape the depression. But in the novels of Aldous Huxley and Evelyn Waugh there did appear a wickedly funny strain of black humor that can only be described as decadent—or as emanating from a decadent sensibility and appealing to a decadent taste. When they got serious, as Huxley did in his "mystical" novels and Waugh in his war trilogy, they could be tiresome, but in novels like *Crome Yellow* and *Decline and Fall,* any serious theme is neatly concealed beneath an unerring satirical wit.

If Graham Greene had not opted so frequently for the seedy and the sensational, he, too, could have qualified as a decadent, for his observations are wry enough, his disdain for the world's vanities lofty enough, and his fascination with Catholicism Wildean enough to afford him the required stance. But, except for *Travels with My Aunt,* Greene is too concerned with religion and politics to be taken *un*seriously. However, in all his works it is not unusual to find the jaded observation, the uncharitable aside, the sardonic humor that are the hallmarks of decadent style. Certainly the diabolical Dr. Fischer of Geneva behaves with an unwholesome degree of decadent panache. His treatment of his guests, who willingly accept humiliation for the sake of greed, is worthy of Des Esseintes and his cynical exploitation of human weakness.

Although I would be reluctant to call anyone as versatile as Tom Wolfe an exclusively decadent writer, I do not hesitate to place him high on the list of modern writers who write about decadent themes. (One collection of his shorter pieces he put together himself is appropriately titled *The Purple Decades!*) There is more than just a trace of decadence in his style, his tone, his point of view, and in the way he presents social reality and human nature in the late twentieth century. As a critic of contemporary culture, he is so embarrassingly accurate, so hilariously funny, and so coolly detached that it takes an effort of the will to bother about the moral premise in his writings—or even to care if there is one.

Wolfe writes like someone who knows life is a zoo but who is getting such a kick out of the antics of the animals that he cannot ruthlessly condemn them. Human folly is his bread and butter, and although he might wish for less of it on principle, in reality he would hate to see it disappear—and seriously doubts that it ever will. His satire is so disarming, it tickles more than it hurts. And no one goes unscathed, not even Wolfe himself. He sees through everything and everybody. But even though his satire is biting and sharp, it is so good-humored that it makes even the silliest characters sympathetic. The world he depicts in *The Bonfire of the Vanities* is one in which inanity reigns supreme. And about the only way to survive this world gone mad, Wolfe implies, is to stand back, poke fun at it, and try not to let it get to you. You can't get much closer than that to the decadent *Weltanschauung.*

Modern decadence may not be the hothouse variety of the 1890s, but it is an enduring force in modern literature. And while few modern works may be cut entirely from the decadent cloth, the threads of decadence are so unmistakably woven into the fabric of so many novels of this century that these strands, once separated from the other, more traditional rhetorics of fiction, can reveal a great deal about how some of our most provocative modern writers respond to a world at the end of a millennium.

Chapter 1:

In Pursuit of Pleasure

> No civilized man ever regrets a pleasure, and no uncivilized man
> ever knows what a pleasure is.
>
> Oscar Wilde, *The Picture of Dorian Gray*

"Never put off till tomorrow the pleasure you can enjoy today," says Uncle
Eustace Barnack in Aldous Huxley's *Time Must Have a Stop* (109). Uncle
Eustace is a caricature of the clones of Oscar Wilde, a comic figure fond of re-
citing limericks like this one:

> There was an old man of Moldavia
> Who wouldn't believe in our Savior
> So he founded instead
> With himself as the head
> The cult of Decorous Behavior (111).

In *Decadence,* philosopher C.E.M. Joad describes the followers of the "cult
of decorous behavior" as people who seek "to have a good time through the
cultivation of the senses and the dedication of the self to the satisfaction of the
self's desires" (76). What Joad is describing, of course, is hedonism, and it was
the hedonism preached by Walter Pater in the late nineteenth century that encouraged his followers to devote themselves to the pursuit of what the French,
always there with the right word, call a *frisson.*

A *frisson* is a thrill, a shudder of delight, a pulse of ecstasy, a jolt of pure joy,
and it was the ambition of the aesthetes of Oscar Wilde's day to measure the
quality of experience by the frequency and intensity with which they experienced such sensations. Pater, their mentor, had spelled it out for them: "A

counted number of pulses only is given to us of a variegated, dramatic life. How may we see in them all that is to be seen in them by the finest senses? How shall we pass most swiftly from point to point, and be present always at the focus where the greatest number of vital forces unite in their purest energy?" (*Renaissance,* 236). To those eager to break the deadlock of Victorian propriety, these questions were challenges, their mandate clear and irresistible.

"To burn always with this hard, gemlike flame, to maintain this ecstasy, is success in life," Pater declared, and this was enough to send his disciples in search of ways to burn. Pater included this epigram in the conclusion to *Studies in the History of the Renaissance,* a work about which Oscar Wilde once said: "It is my golden book. I never travel without it; it is the very flower of decadence: the last trumpet should have sounded when it was written."

Although Pater deleted this inflammatory conclusion from later editions when he became worried about its effect, an effect he swore he never intended, the result was merely to make the challenge all the more attractive. And once this pursuit of the *frisson* had captured the imagination of Wilde's generation, it continued to exercise its influence on the generations that followed. Actually, the impulse had been there all along; it was simply that by the late nineteenth century, at least in England, behind each *frisson* was the added thrill of anti-Victorianism and the image of Mrs. Grundy's stunned expression. Oscar Wilde once quipped that life was nothing but a "bad quarter of an hour made up of exquisite moments." In the twentieth century, that quarter of an hour was to become the "fifteen minutes of fame" Andy Warhol has promised us all.

In response to Pater's overwhelming "How may we . . . ?" and "How shall we . . . ?" decadents have had no trouble finding ways to crowd their lives with a succession of *frissons.* For the most part they have succeeded in burning with a gemlike flame through the cultivation of morally questionable passions and desires, preferring to think that guilt is merely a means of getting more mileage out of your sins.

Duc Jean Floressas Des Esseintes, the neurotic hero of Huysmans' *Against Nature,* has a passion for novelty, for example, which he sets about gratifying in extraordinary and outrageous ways. In fact, Huysmans' novel is organized according to these eccentric distractions, with each chapter devoted to the pursuit of a particular one. Enervated by a lifetime of reckless indulgence, Des Esseintes retreats to a villa in the suburbs of Paris where he lives the life of a sybaritic recluse. Having exhausted the pleasures of the flesh, he now turns to the pleasures of the mind, systematically pursuing and abandoning one *frisson* after another.

"Nature," he declares, "has had her day," and so he tries to escape nature, to transcend nature by seeking gratification in unnatural color combinations, in exotic plants that look artificial, and in art that flirts with the bizarre and borders on the grotesque. He sets his heart on finding exotic pictures steeped in myth and the "aura of antique corruption," pictures utterly removed from the modern world and its tiresome distractions. What he wants are works that release him from the world of the familiar, works that stimulate his nerves, works that excite his imagination by means of arcane associations, esoteric nightmares, and visions both sinister and insinuating. The artist he finally seizes upon, the only one who can satisfy his aesthetic craving, is Gustave Moreau to whose painting of Salome he finds himself drawn night after night. She is an obsession with him, as she was with others of that period, most notably Oscar Wilde in his controversial play that bears her name. Des Esseintes thinks of her as the "symbolic incarnation of undying Lust, the Goddess of immortal Hysteria . . . the monstrous Beast," callous, careless, astonishingly cruel, monstrous in her power to contaminate everything that comes near her, that beholds her, that comes within her poisonous grasp (63–66).

Des Esseintes also experiments with perfumes, fascinated by the fact that fragrances can be produced from raw materials that have nothing to do with the odors they imitate. With patience and determination, he is able to penetrate the mysteries of this neglected art and to understand what he calls its "complex language." Extending the linguistic analogy, he talks of mastering the grammar and syntax of smells and becoming familiar with their dialect so that he can compare the perfumes of the masters by analyzing the sentence structure and the diction of their perfumes (120).

A century later, the art of perfumery achieved literary notoriety in Patrick Süskind's 1986 best-seller, *Perfume,* the story of a man's obsession with smells and his lifelong attempts to capture and recreate them. Although critics have been sparing in their use of the word decadent to describe this extraordinary work, decadent is the only word that sums up the collective critical response used to promote the paperback edition of it. Some call it "elegantly frightening" and "exquisitely shocking" while others say that it "gives off a rare, sinfully addictive chill of pure evil" or that its "sensuous supple prose moves with a pantherish grace." And the central character, Jean-Baptiste Grenouille, is described either as "a most exotic monster" or a "compelling . . . heartless fiend—maddened by an uncaring world" (i–iii).

Grenouille's pursuit of scent is a passion that drives him to possess the essence of everything from the sweat of laborers, to excretions that arouse sympathy, to the smell of a doorknob. Possessing no natural odor of his own, he has an infallible nose for the odors of other things, and he cannot rest until he has isolated all possible smells, unlocked their mystery, analyzed their components, and finally distilled their exact essence.

Each successful distillation is an intense joy for him, *a frisson* that, as it subsides, creates a craving for yet another. His supreme achievement, and ultimately his undoing, is the extraction of the essence of a virgin just at the moment when her sexuality is in first bloom and she is her most seductive, her most voluptuous. The moment Grenouille first inhales that fragrance from a young girl's body, he is overwhelmed with the desire to capture it and maddened by the difficulty of doing so. But he knows there must be a way, and he sets about finding it with total dedication.

Grenouille's only passion, Süskind says, is "the subtle pursuit of scent" (223), and he lets nothing hinder that pursuit. In order to move about undisturbed, he concocts scents that keep others at a distance without their knowing exactly why, and he changes these scents as one might change clothes. Able now to conceal his true nature, he sets about learning how to extract essences from elusive things. He practices first on distilling the scent from a brass doorknob by means of a complicated process involving the use of beef tallow and chalk and infinite patience. If to obtain even a thimbleful of such an essence might require ten thousand doorknobs, he tells himself, it does not matter. He will do whatever it takes, for his plan is to apply this method ultimately to the distillation of the fragrance of virgins.

An eighteenth-century version of a serial killer, Grenouille sets about murdering one virgin after another, carefully selecting his victims for the perfect qualities that his nose unerringly detects and then performing the painstaking ritual of extraction, a process that involves wrapping the body in a greased sheet, letting it "cure" for several hours, and then taking the sheet—along with the girl's hair—back to his quarters where he adds the residue to his growing cache of "pure spirits." Although the procedure might last an entire night, for him the waiting is part of the thrill. He has no trouble staying awake, and in spite of his weariness, he does not mind waiting at all. It is not killing time, for it is active waiting. Even though he might not actually be doing anything, what is happening is, in a sense, "happening through him." He is an artist who has "done his best . . . employed all his artistic skill . . . made not one single mistake. His performance had been unique. It would be crowned with success." This waiting, says Süskind, "filled him with profound satisfaction. . . . He had never felt so fine in all his life, so peaceful" (265).

Aubrey Beardsley is better known for his decadent art than his decadent writing, but he did attempt one short novel that contains most of the elements of decadence, the principal one being the pursuit of pleasure. In *Under the Hill,* Beardsley draws upon the myth of Tannhäuser to celebrate a hero who indulges in a variety of sensual experiences as the guest of Venus and the members of her uninhibited court inside the Venusberg. The supper she gives for him on his first evening in her magic land of pleasure is calculated to titillate the palate as well as the libido, and the dancing that follows is a delight to both eye and ear; but the amorous attentions of Venus that accompany it and the mock seduction that follows are lesser pleasures for him.

More to Tannhäuser's liking, it seems, are his morning ablutions at which he is assisted by a band of young boys who wait in attendance with "warm towels and perfume." The bath itself is by no means an unpleasant experience, but, says Beardsley, it is "in the drying and delicious frictions, that a bather finds his chiefest pleasures," and Tannhäuser obviously enjoys these "quasi amorous functions." In fact, says Beardsley, "the delicate attention they paid his loving parts aroused feelings within him that almost amounted to gratitude" and adds that "any touch of homesickness [Tannhäuser] might have felt before was utterly dispelled" (36–37).

Hedonism connotes excess, and its pleasures can quickly become a curse once passion takes over and gets out of control. Probably the most tragic and certainly the most disturbing example of the curse of uncontrollable passion is to be found in the decline and fall of Gustav von Aschenbach in Thomas Mann's powerful novella, *Death in Venice.* Aschenbach flees Munich for Venice in what is ostensibly an attempt to escape for a while the pressures of fame and a lifetime of severe self-discipline. A man in his fifties, Aschenbach has spent his life pushing himself to the limit to become a highly acclaimed man of letters. All this time he has kept his emotions carefully in check, never allowing himself to surrender to them and thereby jeopardize his literary aspirations.

Now, exhausted and restless, he travels to the seductive south, driven by the legendary Germanic *Streben nach dem Süden,* a longing for the lushness and ease of subtropical climes, particularly for the aesthetic and sensual delights of Italy, the birthplace of the Renaissance. There his fate is sealed in the form of Tadzio, a young Polish boy on holiday with his family, who becomes, in Aschenbach's feverish imagination and weakening resistance, the incarnation of beauty and, so it would seem, the irresistible object of a libidinous fantasy Aschenbach cannot bring himself to acknowledge. Afflicted with the classic blindness of the artist who, like the hero of *Perfume,* can smell every odor but his own, Aschenbach clings to the illusion that his adoration of the boy is his tribute to the ideal of the beautiful. In fact, he is so convinced of the purity of his emotions that he attributes the *frisson* to nature herself, which, he says, "shivers with ecstasy when the mind bows down in homage before beauty" (474).

What Aschenbach does not appreciate, until it is too late, are the subtle ways in which worship of the aesthetic can first weaken and then destroy the worshiper. He knows that "art heightens life [and] gives deeper joy," but he ignores the fact that she also "consumes more swiftly." Referring to such worshipers as "votaries," Mann says that although art "lets them lead outwardly a life of the most cloistered calm, she will in the end produce in them a fastidiousness, an over-refinement, a nervous fever and exhaustion, such as a career of extravagant passions and pleasures can hardly show" (449).

When an outbreak of cholera sends other travelers hurrying home, Aschenbach remains, wholly obsessed with this faun/satyr figure with whom he has no more communication than an occasional bit of cryptic eye contact. Eventually he succumbs to the disease, even seems to welcome it, and finally dies on the beach of the Lido. The last thing his eyes rest on is the figure of Tadzio, standing knee-deep in the water, one arm raised and pointing to what seems like some unattainable destination beyond the horizon. Aschenbach's tragic fate illustrates the ironic way in which the fragility of the pursuer only amplifies the futility of the pursuit.

That destiny subverts the gratification of the passions is also the theme of *The Spoils of Poynton* by Henry James. Mrs. Gareth, the dominant figure in this dark comedy, has an overwhelming passion for furnishings, a passion which she has spent a lifetime cultivating and which drives her to ruin lives, her own among them, in her desperation to hang on to her cherished possessions. Virginia Woolf once complained that Victorian novels were mostly about furniture. In the case of *The Spoils of Poynton,* her observation is accurate, but not in the sense she made it. Her complaint had to do with writers who emphasized material things and interpreted life only in terms of property and possessions. She had writers like John Galsworthy and Arnold Bennett in mind when she said it, novelists whose characters' happiness depends more on what they have than what they are. What James has done, however, is to give us a story that really *is* about furniture, furniture that so dominates the life of one of its characters that it becomes her nemesis and the symbol of treachery and villainy, of pride and possessiveness, and of deadly vanity.

Mrs. Gareth spends her life collecting heirlooms and antiques and *objets d'art* with the zeal of a convert. It is an obsession with her. Gustav Aschenbach could not be more enamoured of the idea of beauty than Mrs. Gareth is of beautiful things, and her goal is not to share them but only to possess them for her pleasure alone. In fact, when her husband's death dispossesses her, and her son Owen inherits Poynton, she literally expropriates the furnishings rather than run the risk of letting them fall into the hands of Mona Brigstock, her son's fiancée. Mrs. Gareth is convinced that Mona could not possibly appreciate them whereas Fleda Vetch, the young woman Mrs. Gareth would like her son to marry, obviously would. But since Mrs. Gareth has only Fleda's word for Fleda's taste, it is much more likely that she sees a chance to dominate mousy little Fleda and regain her rightful place as Mistress of Poynton. The self-centeredness of the decadent is paramount in her character, and the thrill she experiences as she repossesses her precious spoils and outwits Mona is a match for any aesthete's *frisson.*

In being possessed by her possessions and unwilling to let go when they are no longer legally hers, Mrs. Gareth suffers what Joad calls "a levelling of the soul" that ultimately deprives her of the ability to distinguish one pleasure from another. Which does she enjoy more, one wonders: possessing the spoils or keeping them from others? manipulating Fleda or outwitting Mona? This debilitating effect on the very spirit that sought its opposite is one of Joad's main concerns in his study of decadence. He contends that decadents make the mistake of imputing values to things and then fooling themselves into believing that those values are intrinsic. Since their value system, therefore, is based not on values inherent in things but in values arbitrarily assigned to them, it must ultimately fail them. This is precisely what happens to Mrs. Gareth when she reaches the point where controlling the spoils becomes more important than the spoils themselves or the lives of those affected by them.

With the self-awareness that distinguishes the decadent artist from the decadent hero, Oscar Wilde understood the irony of the illusory pursuit of pleasure. Richard Ellmann, in his biography of Wilde, says that Wilde was fully aware of the fact that the pleasures he sought would dissipate and that he would eventually become the victim of the very experiences he pursued. "To fall victim to himself was to bring his experience to the utmost bound," says Ellmann; "unfortunately it was like committing suicide, as Dorian Gray would discover" (270). At one point in *The Picture of Dorian Gray*, Dorian worries aloud that something horrible might happen to him, and Lord Henry tells him that the only horrible thing in the world is ennui, "the one sin," he says, "for which there is no forgiveness" (368). Ennui, Wilde knew, was the ultimate enemy of hedonism. "Live! Live the wonderful life that is in you!" Lord Henry urges Dorian in the way Mephistopheles urged Faust. "Let nothing be lost upon you. Be always searching for new sensations. Be afraid of nothing. . . . A new Hedonism—that is what our century wants. You might be its visible symbol. With your personality there is nothing you could not do" (164).

In "The Devil's Opponent," an unfinished story Isak Dinesen wrote in 1904, there is a situation that parallels the relationship between Lord Henry and Dorian Gray. In the Dinesen story, a young English nobleman comes under the influence of two adventurers in London who have an unlimited "passion for amusement." The older of the two adventurers detects "something sensitive and fine" in the young nobleman's bearing, and this quality arouses "a wicked impulse" in the older man who, Dinesen says, "was sometimes up, sometimes deep down, and who felt at ease in both places" (Thurman, 77). Lord Henry, at home on the heights or in the depths, can likewise not resist the "wicked impulse" to lead Dorian astray.

Lord Henry, of course, does not believe half of what he himself says, but Dorian is overwhelmed by such intoxicating advice and follows it far in excess of anything Lord Henry could ever imagine. This is a good example of the difference between the preaching decadent and the practicing one. Lord Henry says outrageous things for their shock value, not really believing that he will be taken seriously. Still he knows that there is a half-truth in every epigram just as there is a half-truth in every lie, and beneath his offhand remarks there lurks a dark desire to see them heeded.

"We degenerate into hideous puppets, haunted by the memory of the passions of which we were too much afraid, and the exquisite temptations that we had not the courage to yield to" (165), he cries, flaunting the philosophy of the hedonist who finds as much harm in renunciation as in debauchery. Lord Henry's silver tongue lures Dorian into the trap, a trap Lord Henry is too smart to get caught in himself. But to a young man like Dorian, intoxicated with life and just beginning to find his own place in it, Lord Henry's prophecy of a "new Hedonism" is the stuff voluptuous dreams are made of.

Later, when Dorian has turned those dreams into sensual nightmares, the enormity of which is unknown to his mentor, Lord Henry says to him, "You have crushed the grapes against your palate" (383). This is an ironic echo of the line from the famous "Ode on Melancholy" in which Keats writes that none can see melancholy's "sovran shrine" save the one whose tongue "Can burst Joy's grape against his palate fine." The romantic effusion of Keats, terminally ill and still in the flush of youth, smacks of a sort of gallows gallantry, an "eat drink and be merry, for tomorrow we *surely* die" élan. By the time it reaches Dorian, however, it has become the hollow exercise of the profligate who, in Ernest Dowson's words, cries out "for madder music and for stronger wine."

Later, still unaware of the extent of Dorian's depravity, Lord Henry continues to toss off flippant remarks, remarks that begin to take on sinister overtones. As Dorian inwardly cringes, Lord Henry blithely prattles on about how

life is a question of nerves, and fibres, and slowly built-up cells in which thought hides itself and passion has its dream. You may fancy yourself safe and think yourself strong, [he says]. But a chance tone of colour in a room or a morning sky, a particular perfume that you had once loved and that brings subtle memories with it, a line from a forgotten poem that you had come across again, a cadence from a piece of music that you had ceased to play—I tell you, Dorian, that it is on things like these that our lives depend (383).

By this time, however, Dorian knows better. He has just murdered Basil Hallward, the friend who painted his portrait, and been responsible for the suicide of Alan Campbell, a friend he corrupted and then blackmailed into disposing of Hallward's body.

Wilde exemplifies the multiple personalities of the decadent, the "three faces of Satan," as it were, for he saw parts of himself in all three of the central characters in *Dorian Gray:* "Basil Hallward is what I think I am: Lord Henry what the world thinks me: Dorian is what I would like to be—in other ages, perhaps," he once remarked (Ellmann, 319). Dorian is corrupted by decadence, Hallward contaminated by it, Lord Henry its purveyor and shrewdest critic. Lord Henry's pronouncements are parodies, but they are persuasive ones. His is the spirit that informs Wilde's comedies of manners. Hallward's is the spirit of *Salome,* the serious, haunted artist who has found something rotten at the core of life and is too fascinated to look away but fearful enough to keep it at a distance. Dorian is the devil's disciple. He lacks both the wit that restores the spirit and the wisdom that redeems the soul. His is the intemperate spirit of Wilde in his last days, ravaged by debauchery, bereft of hope.

It is as devil's advocate that Wilde could say to André Gide: "Nothing is good in moderation. You cannot know the good in anything till you have torn the heart out of it by excess" (Ellmann, 268). Although Gide was too intelligent not to sense the mockery in much of what Wilde said, he was also too overwhelmed by the novelty of his own sexuality not to take any rationalization to heart. At an age when he was just discovering in himself the same proclivities that were destined to destroy Wilde, he was receptive to any encouragement he could find, especially if it came from someone like Wilde who, until his trial, seemed to be able to flout society's standards with utter impunity.

In *The Immoralist* André Gide created in the personality of Ménalque a character similar to Lord Henry and bearing an unmistakable resemblance to Oscar Wilde. In his biography of Wilde, Richard Ellmann tells of how Wilde influenced André Gide at a critical time in Gide's youth by turning things upside down. Wilde felt that Gide needed to unburden himself of a sterile aestheticism and a restrictive religion, and Wilde's way of helping him was not by rejecting either aesthetics or religion, but by "turning sacred things inside out to make them secular, and secular things inside out to make them sacred." He presented Gide with examples of "souls becoming carnal and lusts becoming spiritual." He preached the new Hellenism, which taught that the aesthetic world was part of, not apart from, experience, and Gide, says Ellmann, felt liberated by it (361).

In *The Immoralist,* Gide recounts how Michel, the main character, discovers and then cultivates his own perverse pleasures. "One morning I had a curious revelation about myself," says Michel and then goes on to describe an incident that occurred to him when he was alone one day in his room in Biskra, Algeria, with Moktir, one of his wife's protégés. Michel tells of how he was leaning on the mantel, pretending to read a book while actually watching the movements of the child in the mirror. "A curiosity I could not quite account for made me follow his every movement," he says. Not knowing he is being watched and thinking that Michel is deep in his book, Moktir slips over to a sewing table, snatches a pair of tiny scissors, and stuffs them into his *burnous.* "My heart pounded a moment," Michel confesses, "but the most prudent rationalization could not produce in me the slightest feeling of disgust. Quite the contrary, I could not manage to convince myself that the feeling which filled me at that moment was anything but amusement, but delight" (44).

After he has given Moktir plenty of time to conceal the scissors, Michel turns to him and acts as if nothing at all has happened. He knows he could pretend that since his wife, Marceline, is quite fond of the child, he is only trying to spare her pain by not denouncing Moktir; but he also knows that that is not his real reason. His real reason is the perverse pleasure he takes in watching himself being robbed by a person who does not know that Michel knows. There is also, obviously, pleasure in being robbed by an Arab boy of whom he is growing a little too fond. As he admits, "From that day on, Moktir became my favorite" (44).

Ménalque has a powerful influence on Michel, a young man fully as narcissistic and, in his own way, almost as depraved as Dorian Gray. Ménalque tells Michel at one point that he loves life too much to sleepwalk through it, that he cherishes "a sense of the precarious" by which he stimulates his life. "I can't say I love danger," he says, "but I love a life of risk, I want life to demand of me, at every moment, all my courage, all my happiness, and all my health" (99). Such talk is music to Michel's ears. He has just experienced a dramatic turnaround in his life, having recently recovered from a long bout with tuberculosis to emerge fit and vigorous and ready to make up for lost time. He has also recently discovered a latent inclination toward certain perverse practices, an inclination that Ménalque's prompting encourages him to exploit. Thus, Michel hangs on to every word with the fervor of an ambitious acolyte as Ménalque tells him of the joys that await him, each to be savored as if it were, for the moment, the only joy. Each joy, he says, is like manna in the desert, which does not last from one day to the next, or like the water Plato tells about that cannot be stored in a pitcher but has to be drunk directly from the fountain. "Let each moment," he says, "carry away whatever it has brought" (112).

In a confession that shows what an eager sorcerer's apprentice he is, Michel admits to a fascination with the figure of the young king Athalaric, a legendary debauchee. "I imagined this fifteen-year-old," he says, "enjoying for a few years with unruly favorites his own age a violent, voluptuous, unbridled life, dying at eighteen, utterly corrupted, glutted with debauchery." On the one hand he equates Athalaric's hunger for excess with his own wild yearnings while on the other he tries to take from the young king's hideous death some lesson for himself. Being torn in opposite directions this way is typical of the dual nature of the decadent personality: on the one side is the willing witness to depravity, on the other its willing victim. The story of young king Athalaric is perfect for the artist looking for a decadent theme but poison for the voluptuary looking for a role model.

Most of Michel's pleasures, however, are passive. In Africa he gets a thrill from merely watching the Arab boy steal the scissors. Later, when he is back at his estate in France, he is excited by the prospect of poachers stealing his own game on his own land as he observes them from a hiding place. Meanwhile, he envies the lack of inhibition, the ability to experience primary sensations that he occasionally detects in others, especially on the part of men he finds physically attractive. Among a group of workmen he is observing one day, one man in particular catches his eye, a tall, good-looking man, "not stupid but guided solely by instinct," a man who, he surmises, does everything "on the spur of the moment," a man who yields "to every passing impulse" (120).

Michel, like Aschenbach, surrenders joyfully to the exaltation of feeling over thought. Once he has recovered his health and discovered his sensuality, he comes to the conclusion that thinking contributes little to feeling and is astonished to discover that within himself "sensation was becoming as powerful as thought." Now that his senses had been awakened, they were taking on a life of their own, "were recovering a whole history, were recomposing their own past. They were alive!" he realizes, "had never stopped living, had maintained, during all those years of study, a latent and deceitful life" (37).

Intoxicated by what he feels is a release from the prison of the mind by virtue of the triumph of the senses, Michel begins to experience the sensations so coveted by the hedonists. "I had forgotten my exhaustion and my discomfort," he says. "I walked on in a kind of ecstasy, a silent happiness, an exaltation of the senses and of the flesh. . . . I had no thoughts: what did thinking matter? With extraordinary intensity, I felt" (39–40).

In the literature that has appeared later in the twentieth century, the pursuit of pleasure without social responsibility has continued to give many works a decadent cast. Similar in spirit to the hedonists of the *fin de siècle* are the party-goers and joyriders of the F. Scott Fitzgerald jazz-age stories or even the Ernest Hemingway expatriates who seek thrills by running with the bulls at Pamplona or by hunting big game in Africa. Fitzgerald, in *The Beautiful and the Damned,* describes the pervading goal of his day as "the final polish of the shoe, the ultimate dab of the clothes brush, and a sort of intellectual There!" (3).

Christopher Isherwood spent much of his life in the shadow of decadence, particularly during his years in Berlin before the rise of the Nazis when he, like Oscar Wilde, "feasted with panthers." For Isherwood, it was the shallow young men of the blue-collar proletariat with whom he mingled while observing the "blue angel" twilight of the Weimar Republic. Historians are quick to point to the artistic vitality of the twenties in Berlin, but it was the parasites on the fringe that Isherwood lived among and wrote about, those who took their pleasure where they found it. Certainly in *Sally Bowles* he caught the mood of self-indulgence that finds its classic expression in the lyrics of the cabaret songs Marlene Dietrich made famous. The self-indulgence of Sally Bowles, like that of Holly Golightly in Truman Capote's *Breakfast at Tiffany's,* has a charm to it that is possibly closer to high spirits than hedonism, but it is not as ingenuous as it seems. Both girls, in looking out for themselves, are looking for pleasure, and they have come to Berlin and New York City respectively to cast off any constraints that might inhibit that pursuit.

There is also a self-indulgent side to Holden Caulfield in J.D. Salinger's *The Catcher in the Rye.* Beyond the routine self-indulgence of adolescent melancholy is Holden's pursuit of his own personal *frisson,* namely the identification of phonies from among the people he comes in contact with, and for him that means just about everybody. Nothing makes Holden happier than to discover that the person he thought might just be genuine is, after all, as phony as everybody else. Actually, this phony-hunting seems original with Holden, but in revealing it Salinger is identifying a trait common to decadents who, as we will see later, need to find some reason to feel alienated and superior. Holden claims that he is not indifferent to human misery, that he wants to be the "catcher in the rye" who stops people from going off the deep end, but his dream is to escape to the woods of Vermont, and this is exactly what Salinger himself chose to do when, in the mid-sixties, he turned his back on the world and went into seclusion.

The late fifties saw the publication of a number of works whose self-indulgent heroes and heroines give these works a distinctly decadent flavor. Earlier in the decade that flavor could be detected in the novels of Paul Bowles and Truman Capote, but Bowles's exotic works were ultimately too bloodless to last whereas Capote's slender confections continue to appeal to a taste for the *outré*. *Other Voices, Other Rooms* and *The Grass Harp* have the atmosphere and settings that suggest that peculiar brand of southern decadence that breeds in swamps and Spanish moss and damp, crumbling antebellum mansions. Later, in *Breakfast at Tiffany's,* the setting and atmosphere are different, but the heroine's peculiar brand of self-indulgent disregard for conventions or for anything outside her orbit came as a welcome antidote to Sartre's injunction that the artist must be involved.

At about the same time, several works appeared that seemed blithely indifferent to social realities in favor of shameless self-gratification. The hedonism of Lawrence Durrell has frequently been commented on, and nowhere is it more on display than in the four volumes of his exotic *Alexandria Quartet,* a tetralogy written in the late fifties that in style and imagination was light-years away from the social realism so popular then, particularly with England's Angry Young Men.

It was also about this time that Vladimir Nabokov sent a *frisson* of naughty delight up the spines of the literati with the publication of *Lolita,* the story of a middle-aged academic obsessed with what he labeled "nymphets," prepubescent girls between the ages of nine and fourteen. Humbert Humbert's pursuit of one in particular, Dolores Maze, whom he prefers to call Lolita, is as far removed from social concerns as anything going on in Durrell's Alexandria. Although Nabokov weaves a tapestry of themes into this unusual novel, one of them being a twist on the Henry James theme of the innocent American girl corrupted by Europeans (*Daisy Miller, Portrait of a Lady*), there is a strand of decadence running throughout this story of an aging lecher's erotic odyssey in pursuit of illicit and illegal passion.

Also taking a page from the hedonists but lacking their style are the thrill-seekers of Jack Kerouac's *On the Road,* those beatniks and dharma bums who crisscross the country in souped-up cars hellbent on finding the elusive "it." The addicts and perverts of William Burroughs's psychedelic *Naked Lunch* are yet another story. Burroughs' surrealistic, drug-induced nightmares, if they are decadent at all, are so primarily because of the intense gratification the author so obviously receives from recounting them. Otherwise, it seems that the depraved behavior of the characters is motivated more by a desire to annoy others than to please themselves. Kerouac, however, manages at times to express the voluptuousness of sensory experience in language that strongly echoes the poetic excesses of which decadents are so fond. "The only people for me are the mad ones," he says in *On the Road,* "the ones who are mad to live, mad to talk, mad to be saved, desirous of everything at the same time, the ones who never yawn or say a commonplace thing, but burn, burn, burn like fabulous yellow roman candles exploding like spiders across the stars and in the middle you see the blue centerlight pop and everybody goes 'Awww!'" (9).

The "me decade" of the seventies obscured the line between refined gratification and raw glut, but in 1986 a book appeared that is refreshingly decadent in the sophisticated tradition of Beardsley and Firbank. *Social Disease* by Paul Rudnick restores the lustre to decadent style by offering no apologies for the unabashed hedonism of its cast of totally self-indulgent characters who devote every moment of the day and night, sleeping and waking, to the pursuit of sensory gratification. The only thing that gives them a moment's pause is the fear that they may not be burning brightly enough, not maintaining a maximum level of ecstasy.

Social Disease revolves around the last days of the New York club scene that flourished in the seventies, and much of the action takes place at the "Club de," a renovated New York movie theatre. This cavernous relic from the golden age of the "movie palace" has become a fun house complete with catwalks and strobe lights, throbbing music and artificial fog—a hangout so exclusive that only those who gain the doorman's reluctant approval are allowed to enter. Inside, those favored few enjoy the ultimate in thrills, one of which is "sharing the loo," an experience that allows both sexes "a tremor of satanic naughtiness, of Freudian hell, of genital riot" (54). The club is not presented as a den of iniquity, however, but simply as a place where one can see and be seen by the right people, a place to escape absolutely the mundane world of daylight and work and boring routine.

The "Club de" has a lot in common with the notorious Studio 54, that "Oz of discos," as *The New York Times* called it, the most popular of the clubs that sprang up during the heyday of the discothèque. Like the "Club de," Studio 54 was also a renovated former movie palace, but its emphasis on drugs and sex was much more blatant. Its emblem was the man in the moon sniffing cocaine, and its clientele was allowed to do anything "so long as it was done with [an] . . . outrageous mixture of style and fantasy," as Gerald Clarke puts it in commenting on this favorite hangout of Truman Capote's in the seventies (510). Capote, he says, thought it was too bad that Proust had not had something like it and that it was a shame that people like Ronald Firbank and Oscar Wilde were not around to enjoy it (511).

The three crazy characters who dominate *Social Disease* are a married couple, Venice and Guy Huber, and their gay sidekick, Licky. Venice and Guy, a

sort of punk version of Barbie and Ken, live only for their nights at the club
and are its reigning monarchs. During the day they sleep the sleep of the pure
at heart, not because they are particularly pure but simply because they are so
good at it. Guy swears that sleeping is what he does best, that he has a real talent for it, that he could easily see it as his life's vocation. Paul Rudnick, who
cites Ronald Firbank as an influence, claims that sleeping is the thing he himself is best at, and he expresses this talent with real feeling in the character of
his charmingly harmless hero. Licky, the Hubers' "maid," is a character who
could have stepped straight out of a Firbank novel. He dresses outrageously,
talks incessantly, and fears only one thing in life—boredom.

When the three of them wind up in a posh, minimum-security prison,
Licky reaches the point where he finally cannot take it anymore and decides to
go along with an escape plan, not because he is being mistreated but simply
because life in the prison, in spite of (or in his case, because of) its country-
club conveniences, is so boring. *Boring.* "Licky had finally said it; he had employed the most damning epithet in his vocabulary. Licky feared boredom. He
would try anything to avoid the mundane, the harrowingly tedious, the con-
vulsively humdrum" (182).

So the three of them escape and return to the city only to find that the
"Club de" has undergone a radical change. The beautiful people have disap-
peared, and the place is full of those who had once been ruthlessly excluded—
those polyester people from New Jersey, the ones with no taste, no style, no
class. Licky is devastated, but Venice and Guy bow to the inevitable and end
up in the middle of the dance floor actually dancing a waltz. As Licky would
say, "Could you die!"

Social Disease is a novel that Des Esseintes would have approved of because it
has much in common with the only book he really admired, the *Satyricon* of
Petronius. What he liked about the *Satyricon,* he said, was that it had been
written "with no thought, whatever people may say, of reforming or satiriz-
ing society, and no need to fake a conclusion or point a moral." The same
could be said of *Social Disease,* which, like the *Satyricon,* depicts "in a splen-
didly wrought style, without affording a single glimpse of the author, without
any comment whatever, without a word of approval of condemnation of his
characters' thoughts and actions, the vices of a decrepit civilization, a crumbling empire" (43–44).

One would think that the muckracking novels of Upton Sinclair, the biting
social satires of Sinclair Lewis, the proletarian sympathies of John Steinbeck,
not to mention the social consciousness of writers like Dos Passos and Farrell
and Odets, would have left no room in the twentieth century for anything but
social propaganda in this "the age of the common man." Fortunately, this has
not been the case. Although those characters who have no redeeming social
values and who seem to live only for pleasure may simply be "taking up space"
in the eyes of the moral bullies, their appearance throughout the pages of
twentieth-century literature has rescued it from a dreariness that makes one

wonder just how valuable some of those so-called redeeming social values really are.

"Nothing succeeds like excess," said Oscar Wilde. Or as modern-day decadents might put it: "Too much is not enough."

Chapter 2:

Pride and Preciousness

"The latest craze among ladies is to gild their tongues; but I
should be afraid," she added diffidently, dipping her banana into
her tea, "of poison, myself!"
                        Ronald Firbank, *The Flower Beneath the Foot*

"To fix the last fine shade, the quintessence of things; to fix it fleetingly; to be
a disembodied voice, and yet the voice of a human soul: that is the ideal of
Decadence," said Arthur Symons in his classic essay, "The Decadent Movement in Literature" (141). Symons flirted with decadence for a while in the
1890s, writing some of that period's most voluptuous poetry, poetry with exotic lines like this concluding line from a poem entitled "Hallucination: I":
"One blood-red petal stained the Baudelaire."

Later Symons turned his back on decadence, saying that while it was "interesting, beautiful, novel," it was really nothing more than "a new and beautiful
and interesting disease" (136). The symptoms of this disease, he said, were "an
intense self-consciousness, a restless curiosity . . . [and] a spiritual and moral
perversity" on the one hand and "an over-subtilizing refinement upon refinement" on the other (135). "An over-subtilizing refinement upon refinement"
is, in fact, a fairly accurate definition of the precious side of decadence.
Preciousness manifests itself in such things as an overly fastidious attention to
ornamentation and decoration and an obsession with appearances, as well as a
preoccupation with style and an acute aversion to bad taste.

In *Death in Venice,* Thomas Mann chronicles the progress of this "new and
beautiful and interesting disease" in his portrait of Gustav Aschenbach, the author who becomes the tragic victim of a fatal attraction to art. Obsessed with
the mystery of beauty, Aschenbach longs to plunder the temple of art and

purloin its secret. On the surface, worshipers of art like Aschenbach may seem uplifted by the intoxication of beauty, may seem to "lead outwardly a life of the most cloistered calm," says Mann, but inevitably art will "produce in them a fastidiousness, an over-refinement, a nervous fever and exhaustion, such as a career of extravagant passions and pleasures can hardly show" (449). There exists in the nature of almost every artist, he says, a "wanton and treacherous proneness to side with the beauty that breaks hearts" (458).

A treacherous proneness to overvalue beautiful things is what motivates Mrs. Gareth in James's *The Spoils of Poynton*. At first it reveals itself in scenes of high comedy that seem to be intended to enlist sympathy for a woman of exquisite taste who finds herself in conflict with a family of Philistines. On the very first page of the novel we find Mrs. Gareth in tears over the wallpaper at Waterbath, the vulgar home of the Brigstocks whose daughter, Mona, is engaged to Mrs. Gareth's son, Owen. Long before her visit to the Brigstocks, Mrs. Gareth has had good reason to wonder how Waterbath will compare to the perfections of Poynton, her own country house. Her worst fears are realized when she finds herself assigned to a room with wallpaper so hideous that she is unable to sleep. Even though she cannot see the wallpaper in the dark, she has only to close her eyes to see it in her mind's eye.

Mrs. Gareth's oversensitive reaction is typical of the aesthetic response to the crimes committed by middle-class decorators in the name of fashion. Wallpaper, for example, was all the rage in late Victorian England, and it was enormously popular with the rising middle classes who plastered their walls with densely flowered patterns that offended those who favored the simplicity of white or solid-colored walls hung with family portraits or understated prints. New middle-class wealth was out to impress, and there could be no impressing without ostentation. Subtlety suffocated amidst all the gingerbread and bric-a-brac, and wallpaper was considered a smart way to cover walls that would otherwise have been, as far as the *nouveaux riches* were concerned, embarrassingly empty.

"Modern wallpaper is so bad," said Oscar Wilde, "that a boy brought up under its influence could allege it as a justification for turning to a life of crime" (Ellmann,193). Shortly before he died, Wilde is reputed to have said, in reference to his room at the Hôtel d'Alsace in Paris: "My wallpaper and I are fighting a duel to the death. One or the other of us has to go" (581).

These are Mrs. Gareth's sentiments precisely. Her life has been devoted to the acquisition of precious things with which to furnish Poynton, and when her husband dies and the home, by law, passes to her son, Mrs. Gareth is utterly devastated, for she is convinced that his fiancée, Mona Brigstock, has no taste and that her installation as Mistress of Poynton would be nothing short of an invasion by the vandals. *The Spoils of Poynton* is the chronicle of Mrs. Gareth's machinations to save her furniture from Mona Brigstock even if it means interfering in three lives. But she is determined to let nothing stand in her way. The "spoils" mean everything to her, more than her son's happiness or even her own welfare.

Early in the novel Mrs. Gareth conspires to have Poynton stripped and all its priceless furnishings squeezed into the small cottage she has been forced to inhabit. Later, in a surprise turn of events, she returns the furnishings to Poynton hoping, apparently, to manipulate Owen into an alliance with Fleda Vetch. The plan backfires, and Owen goes ahead with his marriage to Mona. While Owen and his bride are on their honeymoon, Poynton mysteriously burns to the ground, the result, as far as anyone can tell, of some sort of accident.

There is no question of arson, as far as we know, but there is also no doubt about the fact that James leaves us up in the air with an ending fully as ambiguous as the ending of *The Turn of the Screw* or *The Aspern Papers*. Whatever his intention, two conclusions might be drawn that are of interest in terms of decadence. One, obviously, is that the destruction of the furnishings, like the degeneration of Dorian Gray's portrait, is a moral lesson to Mrs. Gareth (and thus to us) about the folly of storing up treasures on earth. Aside from the fact that James was not given to writing tracts, the trouble with this conclusion is that it assumes that Mrs. Gareth would be devastated by the loss. The other conclusion, one closer in spirit to the decadent overtones in the story, is that even if Mrs. Gareth had nothing to do with the fire (and there is no evidence to suggest that she actually did), it would be in her nature, and in the nature of decadents in general, to prefer to see the spoils destroyed rather than allow them to fall into the wrong hands.

If indeed, this is her attitude, it is not unlike that of Howard Roark, the protagonist of Ayn Rand's *The Fountainhead*. Howard Roark is an architect who values his artistic independence over the plight of the homeless to the extent that he uses dynamite to destroy a low-income housing project that has been built in violation of his design. Although Roark knows that this project would provide shelter for hundreds of homeless people, he is more concerned about the fact that allowing modifications to his design would compromise his integrity as an artist. If Mrs. Gareth had, in fact, set fire to Poynton (in the tradition of Bertha Mason and Mrs. Danvers), no jury of her true peers would ever have condemned her.

In an essay entitled "1880," which appeared in *The Yellow Book* in 1894, Max Beerbohm, with gentle mockery, provides a tongue-in-cheek context for the aesthetic sensibilities of a person like Mrs. Gareth: "Beauty had existed long before 1880," he says. "It was Mr. Oscar Wilde who managed her debut." Anyone who studies the period, he says, has to admit that the "social vogue that Beauty began to enjoy" was due in part to Wilde's influence. Inspired by his intense exhortations and fired by his fervid words, people "hurled their mahogany into the streets and ransacked the curio-shops" in their craving for antiques from the days of Queen Anne. "Dados arose upon every wall, sunflowers and the feathers of peacocks curved in every corner," he says, and "tea grew quite cold while the guests were praising the Willow Pattern of its cup." Not only did women of fashion dress themselves in "sinuous draperies and unheard-of greens," he says, but you could not enter a ballroom anywhere without finding "among the women in tiaras and the fops and the distinguished foreigners, half a score of comely ragamuffins in velveteen, murmuring sonnets, posturing, waving their hands" (Small, 201–202).

Although Mrs. Gareth would not have felt entirely at home in this singular company, she would certainly have appreciated Oscar Wilde's concern about things not "living up to my blue china." Wilde hoped, of course, that outrageous statements like this would gain him the notoriety that might one day translate itself into fame. For the same reason, he took to wearing costumes that gained him publicity. Wearing clothes that run counter to the prevailing styles is a hallmark of decadent preciousness, but while the clothes must necessarily contradict whatever mundane fashions happen to be in vogue, it is absolutely essential that they have style. Otherwise they express ignorance rather than idiosyncrasy.

The white suit seems to be a particular favorite of the decadent who wishes to set himself apart from those who favor severe understatement as well as from those who favor flamboyance. The color white, as a matter of fact, has a special place among the symbols of decadence. Karl Beckson, in his introduction to *Aesthetes and Decadents,* comments that "it is an error to assume that the decade [1890s] was 'yellow'; indeed, the color white—symbol of purity, which despite their protestations, the Decadents yearned for—dominates the literature of the period" (xxxiii). Huysmans says that Des Esseintes advanced his "considerable reputation as an eccentric by wearing suits of white velvet with gold-laced waistcoats and by sticking a bunch of Parma violets in his shirt-front in lieu of a cravat" (27), and Oscar Wilde reminded onlookers of Pierrot when, as an observer noted on one occasion, he was "dressed in white, white from head to foot, from the tall, broad felt hat to his cane, an ivory sceptre with a round top" (Ellmann, 129).

In Tennessee Williams's *Suddenly Last Summer,* white is associated with Sebastian, a homosexual who uses both his mother and a female friend to procure partners for him. He is always seen wearing a white suit, and in the end when he is killed and devoured by a mob of starving children on the beach, he surrenders to this sacrificial ritual dressed in spotless white. In Somerset Maugham's "The Outstation," Mr. Warburton dresses only in white while he is playing out the role of the Edwardian gentleman deep in the jungles of Borneo.

Tom Wolfe, that inimitable critic of modern culture, achieved a certain notoriety in the sixties because he chose to wear white suits at a time when the fashion—indeed, the uniform—was dirty denims, torn T-shirts, and scruffy sneakers. Not that his clothes alone made his reputation, but there are more widely read authors whose faces are much less familiar, even to their readers. In Tom Wolfe's case, his face—and his suit—have become familiar to millions who have yet to read a word Wolfe has written. Wilde would have understood.

In the case of Truman Capote, Wilde would also have understood, and probably applauded. In Clarke's biography of Capote, there is an account of an incident that illustrates Capote's taste for the precious in matters of dress, although in this instance, not for white. Invited to attend a dinner party in the company of his mother and a close friend, Capote emerged from his room wearing "a black velvet suit, a red velvet vest, a ruffled white shirt, and shiny patent leather pumps." The friend thought he looked like someone who was going to a costume ball, and his mother ordered him to change into his gray flannel suit from Brooks Brothers. Reluctantly he went back into his room and changed, but when he returned, he was still wearing his red velvet vest and his patent leather pumps (126).

The elegant bachelor Elliott Templeton, in Somerset Maugham's *The Razor's Edge,* is fussy to a fault in matters of furnishings, dress, and behavior. Elliott is a Europeanized American with a highly cultivated taste and the means to indulge it. His life is totally devoted to refining that taste and moving in the circles where it can be exhibited and appreciated. He is a complete snob, forever courting the favors of the rich and titled and mixing only with people he considers worth knowing. One might call him a "born again" aristocrat, for he has painstakingly acquired his aristocratic bearing and taste, and he upholds the aristocratic tradition in a way most legitimate aristocrats have long since abandoned. Maugham took the character of Elliott Templeton from real life, basing him on a person who graced the salons of Europe between the wars, the last of a breed who, suspecting that there was little behind the mask of life, lived life with style, turning it into a work of art. He is the consummate gentleman, attentive and forbearing, with impeccable manners and a generous heart. But because he is such a snob, he allows himself to suffer any incivility, tolerate any dullness as long as the offender can lay claim to a title or a fortune.

When it comes to furnishings, Elliott is as fussy as Mrs. Gareth and fully as knowledgeable. Shortly before Elliott Templeton dies, Maugham, who appears in the story as its narrator, has occasion to discuss Elliott's failing health with him and what the consequences of it are likely to be. When the subject of heaven arises, Maugham says that "Elliott saw the celestial habitations in the guise of the châteaux of a Baron de Rothschild with eighteenth-century panelling on the walls, Buhl tables, marquetry cabinets and Louis Quinze suites covered with their original *petit point.*" When Maugham, who narrates the story, tells Elliott that he is apt to find the company in heaven very mixed, Elliott, like Miss Malin in Dinesen's "The Deluge at Norderney,"

takes Holy Writ at its word, insisting that "there are class distinctions in heaven just as there are on earth. . . . I have always moved in the best society in Europe and I have no doubt that I shall move in the best society in heaven. Our Lord has said: The House of my Father hath many mansions. It would be highly unsuitable to lodge the *hoi polloi* in a way to which they're entirely unaccustomed. . . . Believe me, my dear fellow . . . there'll be none of this damned equality in heaven" (237–238).

Because of his generous contributions to the church, including the building and outfitting of a small chapel in Italy, the church has somehow managed to find tenuous evidence of noble blood among Elliott ancestors, enough apparently to encourage him to think of himself as the probable descendant of an Italian count. Elliott is sensible enough not to advertise this dubious fact, but he does allow himself the luxury of having a small crown stitched above the monogram on his underclothes and pajamas. And when he dies, he asks to be buried in his Philip II costume—the Count's sword at his side, the Order of the Golden Fleece on his breast—beneath the altar of the chapel he had had built.

This costume, fashioned after one presumably worn by his alleged ancestor, The Count de Lauria, is the one he had hoped to wear to a costume ball being given by a wealthy American widow who has a villa near his on the Riviera. As the day of the party approaches and he does not receive an invitation, Elliott is devastated. Even though he is on his deathbed and totally incapable of attending, not being invited is more than he can bear. The truth is that the hostess has no intention of inviting him because of gossip he has spread about her and her chauffeur, but Maugham, seeing that Elliott is literally heartbroken, filches an invitation and sends it to him, knowing that he is too weak to go but that he desperately needs to feel included. The subterfuge works, and Elliott dies a happy man, but not before he has dictated this note to the hostess: "Mr. Elliott Templeton regrets that he cannot accept Princess Novemali's kind invitation owing to a previous engagement with his Blessed Lord" (239).

In *The Picture of Dorian Gray,* Wilde includes several scenes that illustrate the sort of precious behavior that foreshadows that of Elliott Templeton and which has insinuated itself into the pages of modern literature ever since. In one scene, Lord Henry is lying on a divan of Persian saddle bags, smoking innumerable opium-tainted cigarettes, and admiring the "gleam of the honey-sweet and honey-coloured blossoms of a laburnum, whose tremulous branches seemed hardly able to bear the burden of a beauty so flame-like as theirs." As he lets this experience overwhelm him, he is aware of how the shadows of birds flitting across the silk curtains at the window produce a fleeting Japanese effect "making him think of those pallid jade-faced painters of Tokyo who, through the medium of an art that is necessarily immobile, seek to convey the sense of swiftness and motion" (140).

In another scene one can hear the unmistakable voice of Oscar Wilde in a conversation between Dorian Gray and Basil Hallward in which Dorian insists he is not like the young man who used to say that "yellow satin could console one for all the miseries of life." Dorian maintains instead, in a statement worthy of Mrs. Gareth, that he loves "beautiful things that one can touch and handle. Old brocades, green bronzes, lacquer-work, carved ivories, exquisite surroundings, luxury, pomp, there is much to be got from all these," he says (263). Dorian's most extreme expression of preciousness is prompted by his obsession with Huysmans' *Against Nature*. [Wilde withholds the title of the book, but its identity is obvious from his description of it.] So enamoured is Dorian of this book that he secures from Paris nine oversized editions of it and has them bound in different colors, "so that they might suit [the] various moods and the changing fancies of a nature over which he seemed, at times, to have almost entirely lost control." It is no wonder, then, that he looks upon the book as "the story of his own life, written before he had lived it" (282).

Like his fictional counterparts, Des Esseintes and Jean-Baptiste Grenouille, Dorian applies himself to the study of perfumes, probing the "secrets of their manufacture, distilling heavily scented oils, and burning odorous gums from the East." He is fascinated with the relationship between scents and moods, "wondering what there was in frankincense that made one mystical, and in ambergris that stirred one's passions, and in violets that woke the memory of dead romances, and in musk that troubled the brain, and in champak that stained the imagination." In fact, so involved is he in this pursuit that he has hopes of coming up with a real "psychology of perfumes" which will enable him to analyze the various effects of such sources as "sweet-smelling roots, and scented pollen-laden flowers, of aromatic balms, and of dark and fragrant woods, of spikenard that sickens, of hovenia that makes men mad, and of aloes that are said to be able to expel melancholy from the soul" (290).

Dorian is also fascinated by jewels, another passion he shares with Des Esseintes who gets so carried away by his obsession that he arranges to have the shell of a live tortoise encrusted with a pattern of precious stones. He even manages to procure the services of a jeweler willing to indulge him in this eccentric and expensive whim. As he watches the abused animal drag this heavy burden across the carpet, Des Esseintes gets a curious pleasure out of seeing the way the stones catch the shifting light, but before long the weight proves too much for the tortoise, and it dies. In Evelyn Waugh's *Brideshead Revisited,* there is a similar episode in which Julia's fiancé Rex gives her a diamond-encrusted tortoise as a Christmas gift only to have it disappear—and presumably die—somewhere in the recesses of Brideshead Castle. Dorian is so enthralled by jewels that he has extensive collections of various stones, and he sometimes spends whole days doing nothing but playing with them, arranging and rearranging them in their cases (291). At one point he attends a costume ball dressed as a French admiral in a uniform covered with five hundred and sixty pearls.

It is also part of decadent preciousness to display a self-conscious fastidiousness about food, or more precisely, about the setting in which food is served. Assisted by Lord Henry, Dorian Gray gives little dinners that are famous for the care with which he places his guests and the exquisite taste he displays in the way he decorates his table "with its subtle symphonic arrangements of exotic flowers, and embroidered cloths, and antique plate of gold and silver." The younger men among his guests see in Dorian the embodiment of an ideal they had hoped to encounter at Eton or Oxford but never did, "a type that was to combine something of the real culture of the scholar with all the grace and distinction and perfect manner of a citizen of the world," one whose life, over-refined by the worship of beauty, had become, itself, a work of art, a life for which "all the other arts seemed to be but a preparation" (284–285).

The infamous "funeral feast" that Des Esseintes hosts in *Against Nature* is probably the most extreme example of the decadent elevation of the ingestion of food to an elaborate ritual of precious dimensions. It is a feast similar, except in one important respect, to the ones he used to serve in his earlier days of de-bauchery just before his health declined and he was forced to move to the country. The difference in this case is that this one is to be a "funeral banquet in memory of the host's virility, lately but only temporarily deceased" (27). He therefore insists on an ebony motif. Outside he has the garden paths strewn with charcoal and the ornamental pond edged with black basalt and filled with ink. He also has all the shrubberies dug up and replaced with cy-presses and pines. Inside, in a dining room draped in black, he arranges to have the dinner itself served on a black cloth on which there are baskets of violets and other purplish flowers while black candles cast an eerie purplish half-light from the candelabra and the chandeliers.

While a concealed orchestra plays funeral marches, the guests are served by "naked negresses" and dine off "black-bordered plates." The menu consists of turtle soup, rye bread, ripe olives, caviar, black puddings, licorice-colored sauces, truffle jellies, dark chocolates, plum-puddings, nectarines, pears in grape syrup, mulberries, and black cherries. Only dark wines like port are served during dinner, and afterwards there is black coffee and a walnut cordial (27).

In November of 1966, Truman Capote threw a party that for sheer imagi-nation and attention to detail would make any decadent proud. This party has been hailed as the party, not just of the decade, but of the century. In its con-ception and implementation, it had many interesting decadent touches, not the least of which was the enormous but engaging ego of its host who planned it with the skill of a military strategist.

In his biography of Capote, Gerald Clarke details the care with which Capote drew up the guest list and dictated the terms. The five hundred guests were to be carefully selected only from among people he knew and liked. This meant that he would not invite a husband and wife unless he approved of both. It also meant that single men and women would have to attend unescorted. Since he knew this might create a problem, he arranged a number of small dinner parties to be held earlier in the evening so that guests could then arrive at his party in groups. Naturally, he decided who should host these dinners and who should be invited to which.

His party was really more of a ball, and it was to begin at ten at the Plaza Hotel, a hotel that, in Capote's opinion, "had the only beautiful ballroom left in New York" (370). It soon came to be known as the Black and White Ball because Capote required all guests to dress only in black and white, an idea he got from Cecil Beaton's Ascot tableau in *My Fair Lady.* He even tried to go so far as to specify "diamonds only," but he was advised against it for the reason that some of the poorer women on his guest list might not be able to come— unless, of course, they begged, borrowed, or stole, a possibility Capote found charming. Nevertheless, he deferred to prudence and abandoned the idea. He did, however, insist that everyone wear a mask, and it was this final touch, the allure of a *bal masqué,* that set the social world agog.

Famous designers were kept busy for weeks creating gowns and masks, but on the night of the ball it was Capote himself who stole the show with a deftly decadent touch. He announced to those clustered around him in their expensive and elaborate masks that his, which they were all admiring, was just a simple Halloween mask he had picked up in a dime store for thirty-nine cents.

The ball was an unqualified success, and yet it cost Capote relatively little to give it, partly because, except for the champagne, he spent very little on food. The midnight buffet was modest by any standards: "chicken hash, spaghetti bolognaise, scrambled eggs, sausages, pastries and coffee" (377), hardly Des Esseintes's exotic dishes or Babette's famous feast! But it was the sort of spare fare only a confident decadent could get away with, reminiscent, in its simplicity, of the legendary New York restaurant known as "The Dungeon," a gloomy eatery that featured prison decor and advertised "fine breads and waters."

Critics of Capote's ball could explain neither the frenzy of the invited nor the furor of the excluded. Other than the sheer imagination he displayed in orchestrating it, the best explanation is probably to be found in the inimitable personality of the host himself, that eccentric, gifted, totally unique elf, a Merlin, as he used to be known, who, like Oscar Wilde, had the uncanny ability to hold people in thrall, to charm them into filling the unfillable void if only until midnight and the mask dropped. Capote was the wizard of the precious touch.

Preciousness can be a matter of prose as well as pose where decadence is concerned. It is most obvious in the mannered style of Aubrey Beardsley and Max Beerbohm and Cyril Connolly, but it reaches its zenith in the spun-sugar delicacy of Ronald Firbank. There is a scene in *The Flower Beneath the Foot* in which Firbank describes "his Weariness, the Prince" as a young man "handsome to tears," whose face "even as a child had lacked innocence. His was that *magnolia* order of colouring," says Firbank, "set off by pleasantly untamed eyes, and teeth like flawless pearls." His Weariness has just returned from the railway station where he had gone to welcome some royal travelers. When asked about them he murmurs, "'They're merely dreadful,' in a voice extinct with boredom" (14).

Elsewhere Firbank refers to "his Lankiness, Prince Olaf," as "a little boy wracked by all the troubles of Spring" (22), and he says of another character that, "swathed in towels, it was delicious to relax his power-balanced limbs upon a comfy couch" (96). He describes a duchess as "raising indolently an almond to her sinuously-chiselled lips" (27). And when a certain Madame Wetme awaits the arrival of the duchess for tea, Firbank writes that she had "whitened her face and rouged her ears, and set a small, but costly aigrette at an insinuating angle in the edifice of her hair." When time drags on and the duchess does not appear, the tension and strain cause "even the little iced-sugar cakes upon the tea-table [to look] green with worry" (74).

Being overly fastidious in matters of prose style is a common characteristic of decadent preciousness. Truman Capote, as precious as he was precocious, claimed the fastidious Flaubert as his mentor, but there was also, in the way he went about his craft, something in him of Oscar Wilde who, according to Richard Ellmann, "pretended to outdo Pater in fastidiousness." "I was working on the proof of one of my poems all morning," Wilde once said to a friend, "and took out a comma." "And in the afternoon?" asked the friend. "In the afternoon? Well, I put it back again" (221).

There is no better indication than this of how far the decadents are removed from their romantic roots. The romantics believed in bursts of inspiration that produced great poetry in first drafts; at least that was the face they showed the world. The world-weary decadents go the other way and boast of the care with which they hone and polish their slight but flawless creations. In *The Decadent Dilemma,* R.K.R. Thornton calls the decadent period in England an "age of afterthought, of reflection" and says that while such refinement has the virtue of "much and careful meditation upon life, its emotions, and its incidents," it also has the vice of "over subtilty and of affectation, when thought thinks upon itself, and when emotions become entangled with the consciousness of them" (41). Times have not changed. According to Gerald Clarke, Capote "endlessly deliberated over such basics as structure and order: he could spend hours examining a single paragraph, like a diamond-cutter deciding how to transform a rough and homely stone into a glittering jewel: and with some exceptions, he constantly and compulsively revised what he had already written" (223–224). This may be why his descriptions of celebrities display a rare talent for capturing, with stunning accuracy, the essence of a person in the prose style itself.

His description of Isak Dinesen in her last years is as exotic as was the wraith-like Dinesen herself. On his way back from the Soviet Union where he had traveled with a touring company that was performing *Porgy and Bess,* Capote stopped off in Denmark to visit Dinesen at Rungstedlund, her seaside villa north of Copenhagen on the road to Elsinore. In *The Dogs Bark,* his account of that tour, he had this to say about her:

The Baroness, weighing a handful of feathers and fragile as a *coquillage* bouquet, entertains callers in a sparse, sparkling parlor sprinkled with sleeping dogs and warmed by a fireplace and a porcelain stove: a room where she, an imposing creation come forward from one of her own Gothic tales, sits bundled in bristling wolfskins and British tweeds, her feet fur-booted, her legs, thin as the thighs of an ortolan, encased in woolen hose, and her neck, round which a ring could fit, looped with frail lilac scarves.

Of her face he says that

a face so faceted, its prisms tossing a proud glitter of intelligence and educated compassion, which is to say wisdom, cannot be an accidental occurrence; nor do such eyes, smudges of kohl darkening the lids, deeply set, like velvet animals burrowed in a cave, fall into the possession of ordinary women (359–360).

To his surprise and dismay, Dinesen took offense at this description, calling Capote "ungallant" and threatening to withdraw her offer to write the introduction to the Danish edition of *Breakfast at Tiffany's,* but she eventually forgave him and wrote it anyway (Clarke, 307).

No contemporary writer can surpass Paul Rudnick when it comes to matching precious style with precious object. In *Social Disease,* he says of Licky that it was his ambition "to become a still photograph, a glossy 8 × 10 processed by a master retoucher," and that to achieve this goal "he sought the ideal pose." On one occasion, he dressed up in "an effortless cream flannel suit, of an Oxford bag; he had placed three bright yellow Ticonderoga pencils in the breast pocket, just because." He calls Licky "attitude incarnate" and adds that to get an idea of what he looks like, all one has to do is "picture an extremely well-dressed exclamation point" (11).

In another scene in the novel, its hero, Guy Huber, is hoping that the pair of zebra shoes he plans to buy "will convince his parents that he is justified in being overdrawn on his account." He describes the shoes as "ethereal," what with their "pointed toes, side laces, a modified Cuban heel, and those primal stripes." The shoes are, in fact, such "perfection" that Guy is almost afraid to wear them and thinks that maybe "he would just keep the shoes in their box, and look at them, the way art collectors visit their Leonardo sketch in the vault." To Guy, such shoes are "beyond wrangling, beyond niggling debate. How," he wonders, "could his parents refuse?" (46) (Incidentally, they do.)

"It is only shallow people who do not judge by appearances," Oscar Wilde once wrote to a friend. "The mystery of the world is the visible, not the invisible." Licky reveals how well he understands this sentiment when he laments the lack of people capable of appreciating the mystery of the superficial.

"Where were the people who know just how to cover their faces when the photographers arrive and yet still be recognized in the picture?" he asks.

Where were the people willing to spend their last three thousand dollars on two yards of fabric? The people who care deeply about the correct way to lean against an archway? The people who talk about sex in terms of trends? Where were the people who, given a choice between a poor haircut and the loss of a loved one, would need a minute? (190).

In his biography of Oscar Wilde, Richard Ellmann refers to a passage in "The Decay of Lying" that could serve as a postscript on preciousness. In this passage Wilde speaks of a club called "The Tired Hedonists." We who belong, he says "are supposed to wear faded roses in our buttonholes when we meet, and to have a sort of cult for Domitian." When someone suggests that the members of the club must be bored with one another, Wilde agrees. "We are," he says. "That is one of the objects of the club."

   And so, says Ellmann with a twinkle in his prose, "Wilde smiled decadence away" (302). Well, not quite.

Chapter 3:

Supping with the Devil

> For I have lived long enough, by now, to have learned, when the
> devil grins at me, to grin back.
> Isak Dinesen, "The Deluge at Norderney"

To the decadents, nothing is sacred. Piety brings out the worst in them—or
the best, depending on your point of view. Part of this irreverent attitude
stems from the fact that decadents are irresistibly inclined to go against the
grain, for they see hypocrisy everywhere and are simply unable to accept it or
ignore it. "Perversity," says Susan Sontag, "is the muse of modern literature"
(*Against,* 53).

Beneath this disdain for the world's pretensions is a feeling of despair born
of the unshakeable suspicion that religion has reneged on its promises. If God
does exist, He has been done a disservice by those who claim to be His good
and faithful servants. Thus, decadent irreverence toward religious matters is,
at least in part, a way of provoking God to show his hand. That this irreverence is also prompted by the urge to amuse or shock cannot, of course, be de-
nied; but as surely as gallows humor betrays fear, religious irreverence betrays
doubt.

In Evelyn Waugh's comic masterpiece *Decline and Fall,* a dour academic by
the name of Mr. Prendergast, in the course of explaining his own cheerful despair, offers what amounts to a plausible explanation for the basis of decadent
irreverence. Mr. Prendergast admits to having *doubts* and, when pressed to
elaborate, exclaims in hoarse disbelief: *"I couldn't understand why God had made
the world at all"* (38). This is the question decadents ask: not what does life
mean but why did God bother? For it is true that while decadents may not
doubt the existence of God, they do doubt the wisdom of creation. Decadent

irreverence, therefore, is not the strident cry of the atheist or the bluster of the believer pushing his luck. Nor is it the blasphemy of cross burning and devil worship and black masses. The weapon of decadent irreverence is humor, and its target is not faith but humbug.

In Isak Dinesen's "The Dreamers," one of the *Seven Gothic Tales,* the story-teller Mira Jama says: "I have been trying for a long time to understand God. Now I have made friends with him. To love him truly you must love change, and must love a joke, these being the true inclinations of his own heart" (355). This is Dinesen's way of reminding us that humor is divine and that God Himself may well prefer a little good-natured ribbing to a lot of unctuous adoration.

Although decadents are notoriously irreverent about everything from motherhood to minimum-security correctional facilities, their favorite sport is, not surprisingly, religion. When Lord Henry Wotton gives Dorian Gray a copy of *Against Nature,* Dorian may call it a "poisonous book," but he also maintains that it is a book that could just as easily have come from the lives of the saints. He confesses that while he was reading it, he was never quite sure whether he was reading "the spiritual ecstasies of some medieval saint or the morbid confessions of a modern sinner" (281).

While *Against Nature* is, indeed, the confessions of a modern sinner, the life of that sinner bears a strong resemblance to the life of a medieval saint, at least on the surface. Cloistered in his suburban sanctuary, Des Esseintes follows a routine that simulates clerical ritual. For example, he receives tradesmen in a lofty hall which he has fitted up to resemble the interior of a church. After he has seated these tradesmen in a row of church stalls, he climbs into a pulpit and preaches a sermon on dandyism, instructing his bootmakers and tailors in matters of fashion and threatening them with monetary excommunication if they do not follow explicitly the instructions he reads to them from his "monitories and bulls."

His mockery of church ritual also extends to the way he furnishes his bedroom to look exactly like a monastery cell. However, he is much too fastidious to put up with the shabbiness of the real thing. Instead he approaches the task as one might approach a stage set, except that in this case, rather than using cheap fabrics to give the illusion of finery, he uses costly materials to give the illusion of rags. The point is to have a bedroom that looks like a genuine Trappist's cell but which is, of course, nothing of the sort. Using saffron silk and strips of kingwood, a dark brown wood with a purple sheen, he is able to simulate the crudity of the monk's cell. To give the effect of plaster, he uses white holland on the ceiling; and to give the illusion of cold floor tiles without the discomfort, he uses a carpet patterned in red squares, dyed white in those places to make it look faded and worn by the tread of sandals and boots.

His bed is a mock hermit's bed made of old wrought iron, highly polished, and his night stand, which had once been an antique priedieu, now contains a chamber pot. Against one wall there is a churchwarden's pew, and the room is lighted by real wax candles in altar candlesticks. Alone in this curious cell, Des Esseintes can imagine that he is far away from Paris and the world and living in the depths of some remote, secluded monastery. The illusion is easy for him to sustain since the life he lives is very similar to the life of a monk minus, of course, the disagreeable routine. He enjoys the best of both worlds, Huysmans tells us, since he is able to enjoy all the benefits of a cloistered life without suffering any of its disadvantages; namely, "the army-style discipline, the lack of comfort, the dirt, the promiscuity, the monotonous idleness" (76).

At the end of *Against Nature*, Huysmans makes it clear that Des Esseintes's behavior, including his irreverence, is a result of profound religious doubt. Shortly before the novel ends, Huysmans writes about his hero's "hunger for religion" and says that he "passionately craved" faith but that "doubts crowded into his fevered mind, upsetting his will" and causing him to reject "on the grounds of common sense . . . the mysteries and dogmas of the Church" (215). The prayer with which the novel concludes is even more disturbing in light of the life Des Esseintes has led up to that point and the desperation that has brought him to his knees. In this prayer he begs the Lord to take pity on the Christian who is troubled by doubts and on the unbeliever who longs to believe, and he compares himself to a galley slave who puts out to sea all alone, in the dark of night, under a sky "no longer lit by the consoling beacon-fires of the ancient hope!" (220).

Religious irreverence takes a different form in Aubrey Beardsley's *Under the Hill,* a novel that, according to Mario Praz in *The Romantic Agony,* "contains the essence of the English Decadent school" (356). When he completed Beardsley's unfinished novel in 1958, John Glassco added a wry account of Tannhäuser's encounter with an intractable pope from whom Tannhäuser hopes to receive absolution. Feeling contrite after a prolonged debauch in the Venusberg, Tannhäuser decides to go to Rome and throw himself at the mercy of the Holy Father. He has vowed to go barefoot all the way, but when he discovers how uncomfortable it is and how long it will take, he manages to satisfy the letter of his vow by riding in his carriage with his shoes off. The Pope is on to him at once and declares that the papal walking stick would have to sprout leaves before His Holiness will ever consent to grant Tannhäuser absolution.

No sooner has Tannhäuser left Rome in dejection than, to the Pope's chagrin, the papal walking stick actually does begin to sprout. Immediately the Pope sends for Tannhäuser, but it is too late. Tannhäuser has returned to the Venusberg where he asks to be hanged for his unabsolved sins. Preparations are made immediately for the hanging and, when everything has been arranged, Tannhäuser is, in fact, hanged. But after a few moments, to his utter surprise (and blessed relief), he returns to life. When he asks for an explanation, Venus tells him that she was only having a little fun with him. There is, she informs him, no death in the Venusberg. Tannhäuser will now have to spend eternity among its delightful iniquities. This may seem like a pretty heavenly version of hell, but if the punishment for sin is endless sinning, then Beardsley's joke may have a hook to it.

Throughout decadent literature there are characters who, for reasons that have little to do with religion, are attracted to the priesthood. Wilde tells us that even Dorian Gray had entertained the idea. In *The Flower Beneath the Foot,* Ronald Firbank tells of a young man named Eddy Monteith who indulges in religious fantasies and had, at one time, been about to join a Jesuit order and enter a monastery. In fact, so much did he admire priestly attire that he had already been sitting for a portrait of himself dressed in a monk's habit until amused friends and horrified relatives talked him out of it.

Nazianzi, the heroine of this novel, feels drawn to orders for reasons that are also not wholly spiritual. Her impulse to take the veil is prompted more by her wish to be close to a nun she idolizes than by the summons to a vocation. That her religious fervor is more secular than spiritual is clear from the prayer she offers at one point in which she calls upon heaven to allow her to "be decorative and to do right" and to "always look young, never more than sixteen or seventeen—at the *very* outside." She also thanks God for creating Yousef, her lover, and prays that he will love her as much as she loves him "especially when he wags it! I mean his tongue," she says. Her prayer ends with a request that God "bless all the sisters at the Flaming-Hood" and that she herself be shown the straight path and kept forever free "from the malicious scandal of the Court: Amen" (50).

Firbank's novels are littered with irreverent throwaway lines that have to be read in context to be truly appreciated. But there is one line in *The Flower Beneath the Foot* that in its own frivolous way captures the spirit of the decadent attitude towards religion. "O, the charm, the flavor of the religious world!" Firbank exclaims. "Where match it for interest or variety!" (135)

It is a comment worthy of Licky in *Social Disease,* a novel in which the author frequently uses religious references irreverently. Licky, we are told, is a sworn foe of silence and, therefore, has taken a vow of chatter the way Trappists vow never to speak. And Guy Huber, the novel's main character, thinks of himself as "the lone Jesuit" whose duty it is at dawn to open the gate to the holy shrine (100) while his wife, Venice, describes herself as feeling like one of those statues that gets carried through village streets in Italy on religious holidays (105). Rudnick even refers to the superthin society women (the ones Tom Wolfe calls "X-rays") as "fetish dieters [with] the figures of El Greco Christs, pinched and tucked and taut" (94).

Elsewhere Rudnick has an irreverent tongue in his cheek when he comments that Guy imagines God to be a sort of "omniscient Jamaican housekeeper . . . shooing away evil and providing treats" (156). And earlier, when Guy is faced with the unhappy prospect of finding a job, his attitude is that it would be nothing short of heresy for him to do anything approaching honest labor since it would be blatant opposition to the will of God (51). Later, when Guy goes to prison, he has a few minutes to kill before meeting his fellow inmates, and since there is a Gideon Bible in his "cell," and he has never read the Bible, he wonders if he has time for a "quick skim." The moment he opens the book, however, he recalls immediately the reason why he has never read the Bible and why that reason justifies his lifelong resistance to Christianity: "terribly small type" (163).

Isak Dinesen's irreverence takes the form of challenging common religious assumptions either by inverting them or by interpreting them in radically new ways. Miss Malin Nat-og-Dag, the elderly spinster of "The Deluge at Norderney," the first story in *Seven Gothic Tales,* is described as "a lady of strictest virtue [who] believed herself to be one of the great female sinners of all time" (9). She boasts of a past of "colossal licentiousness" and believes herself to be the "great whore of Revelation." Her reason for thinking of herself as a notorious adulteress is based on the Biblical passage which says that a man who lusts after a woman in his heart has as much as committed the act. And since she is sure that dozens of young men have, at one time or another, desired her favors, as far as she is concerned the thought has become the deed (21).

Adultery is not the only sin to which Miss Malin willingly confesses. In her imagination she has committed them all. However, unlike the repenting sinner who washes the stains until his sins are made white as wool, Miss Malin takes the greatest pleasure in seeing to it that her wool is dyed a veritable rainbow of deadly hues. This formidable lady is the heroine of all her own fantasies, galloping through the seven deadly sins with the ecstasy of a little boy on a rocking horse determined to win a difficult race. She is troubled by neither fear nor conscience, a bold sinner who, unlike the craven Mary Magdalene who must "retire to the desert of Libya in the company of a skull," prides herself on carrying the weight of her sins with the "skill of an athlete" (22).

In this story, four flood victims are trapped in a barn that is gradually being inundated. In addition to Miss Malin and a young couple, there is an older gentleman who presents himself as a cardinal of the Catholic church. During the course of the story, the Cardinal comes up with a few interesting inversions of his own, inversions that could easily be said to come perilously close to blasphemy. When Miss Malin asks him if he believes in the fall of man, he replies that, while he is convinced that there has been a fall, it is, he thinks, not of man but "of the divinity." An inferior dynasty has seized power, de declares, comparing the revolution in heaven with the French Revolution and its aftermath. The world is no longer in the hands of an absolute monarch, he says, but merely a banal and bourgeois king who possesses all the boring virtues of a model citizen and who lays claim to no divine rights "except by virtue of his virtues" (58).

The problem, as he sees it, is that a God whom we "elect," as it were, is subject to *our* laws rather than we to His, and is forced to conform to *our* ideas of right and wrong. He is appalled by this democratization of heaven, arguing that we can no more demand a moral attitude of God than we can hold a true king responsible to the laws that govern his subjects. "The humane God," he points out, "must share the fate of the bourgeois King" (58). Such a fate is anathema to the Cardinal, who, like Dinesen herself, prefers the God of justice to the God of mercy, the God of Job, not Jude. The Cardinal explains to Miss Malin that he had been brought up to have faith in a humane God and that it had been intolerable to him. Then he tells her of a moment once long ago in Mexico when he experienced a unique kind of spiritual revelation that opened his eyes to the fact that, try as we might to fashion God in our own image, God Himself "does not give a pin for our commandments" (58).

When he tells Miss Malin that the two of them are dying for a lost cause, she insists that they will both certainly get their reward in Paradise, but the Cardinal is not so sure. A bourgeois God, he tells her, will favor bourgeois followers over the old nobility. When she asks him if this means that they must abandon all hope of heaven, he invites her to speculate on how eager she would be to get in there if she were to be given a sneak preview of the place. "It must be the rendezvous of the bourgeoisie," he tells her. "You and I, Madame, . . . shall cut a finer figure in hell. We were trained for it" (58–59).

Later on in the story, the conversation turns to the subject of truth, and Miss Malin declares that she "will take pains to disregard the truth." When the Cardinal objects, Miss Malin asks him where on earth he ever got the idea that God wants the truth from us. She finds it a most extraordinary idea, claiming that God knows the truth already and probably even finds it a trifle dull. "Truth is for tailors and shoemakers," she declares (24) in an observation reminiscent of "The Decay of Lying," in which Oscar Wilde laments the decline of lying (i.e., imagination) in favor of the futile pursuit of illusory truth. Miss Malin's statement is also very much like the comment that Blanche DuBois makes about truth in Tennessee Williams's *A Streetcar Named Desire:* "I don't tell truth," she says. "I tell what *ought* to be truth" (117).

Miss Malin argues that God has always expressed a taste for masquerades, reminding the Cardinal that the Church has routinely referred to human tribulations as blessings in disguise. And so they are, she agrees, but the disguises, she insists, are not just accidental concealments but rather the work of an unrivaled expert. "The Lord himself," she says, "seems to me to have been masquerading pretty freely at the time when he took on flesh and dwelt amongst us" (25). Had she herself been the hostess of the wedding of Cana, she adds, she might have resented the fact that the carpenter's son, whom she had invited in order to treat him to her best wine, had seized the opportunity to change ordinary water into a far finer vintage (24–25).

The Cardinal carries the idea of the masquerading of the Lord a step further by suggesting the possibility that the ultimate moment of truth will arrive when the Lord is revealed to *us,* not we to Him. Perhaps, suggests the Cardinal, the day of judgment will not be the day of reckoning as described by uninspired preachers who imagine it as a day on which all our petty and pathetic attempts at deceit will be unveiled. After all, he argues, God knows about these things already. His prediction is that the day of judgment will, instead, be "the hour in which the Almighty God himself lets fall the mask" (26).

The Catholic church has long been a favorite target of decadent disrespect, partly because of its high visibility, but mostly because of the love-hate relationship decadents have always had with Catholicism. Huysmans returned to the Catholic church late in life, and Oscar Wilde converted to Catholicism on his deathbed. Arnold Hauser calls decadents "hedonists with a bad conscience, sinners who throw themselves . . . into the arms of the Catholic Church" (*Social,* 889). Many of the names that appear in this study are of writers who have either returned to or been converted to Catholicism, including some who have become modern Catholicism's most notable devil's advocates.

David Lodge is an English Catholic writer who enjoys poking fun at the problems of modern Catholics who are trying to survive the impact of Vatican II and the ecclesiastical reforms that, for many of them, have come too late to ease the burden of too many children and too much guilt. Perhaps Lodge's most delightful irreverence occurs in *Souls and Bodies,* a novel that traces the lives of ten British Catholics from the early fifties through Vatican II and beyond. Along the way he commiserates with Catholics struggling to accommodate the rapidly shifting values of both the real and the religious worlds—and failing miserably at it—by taking to task a church that has come to resemble the stock exchange in the way its moral index seems to fluctuate according to the whims of the marketplace. At one point, an English nun who has joined an order in Texas is described as coming down to breakfast in curlers, mumbling a hasty prayer ("Good food, good meat, good God, let's eat!") and then hurrying out to a limousine that is waiting to whisk her and her mini-skirted companions to their "jobs" in downtown Dallas.

Sometimes decadent irreverence in religious matters seems to be an attempt to goad God into retaliating, to dare Him to hurl a thunderbolt or two just to prove that He does after all draw the line somewhere. Certainly when Graham Greene pushes faith to the breaking point, he is bullying God, trying to see how far he can go. In *The Heart of the Matter,* Scobie does not want to hurt the feelings of either his wife or his mistress by having to choose between them, so he commits suicide. However, in order to spare his wife the further pain of believing that he has died in sin, he contrives to make it look as if he died from natural causes. Even though he compounds the sin of adultery with the sin of suicide, he harbors some hope of grace because his suicide is motivated by a compassion which, to him, exceeds God's own.

In *A Burnt-out Case,* a novel set in a leper colony in Africa, Greene suggests that man's morality may be greater than God's mercy. Certainly the compassion Dr. Colin feels for the lepers, a compassion that manifests itself in the doctor's tireless treatment of those afflicted, is a rebuke to a God for allowing disease and suffering to exist in the first place. Greene is able to equate physical suffering with spiritual suffering and thus force the issue to a somewhat uneasy spiritual resolution, but not before Querry, a burnt-out hedonist and spiritual leper, dies at the hands of a fanatically religious husband who falsely accuses Querry of adultery. By the end of the novel Greene has effectively inverted conventional religious assumptions by setting up a situation in which traditional concepts of sin and redemption are put to the test and God Himself is challenged to defend what he has wrought.

In a lighter mood—but an equally serious vein—Greene puts faith to the test in *Monsignor Quixote,* a comic masterpiece set in Spain, in which a Catholic priest and a Communist mayor join forces to evade the authorities who are pursuing them for obscure political reasons. Most of the humor in the novel arises from the fun Greene has at the expense of church doctrine and protocol. In truth, it is not God but the Church that is mocked, for one of Greene's major themes has always been the way in which institutions are in constant danger of becoming inimical to their own principles. Thus the irreverence is a means of seeing through the obstacles that the Church often unwittingly places between the faithful and their beliefs.

When Quixote, who has been virtually defrocked, celebrates mass in pantomime, Greene's irreverence is transformed into a higher form of reverence. There is a parallel here with the "whisky priest" of *The Power and the Glory,* a scapegrace whose saving grace is his unshakeable faith and his compassion. When he is summoned to hear the confession of a notorious gangster, he goes without hesitation, even though he knows it means delivering himself up to his enemies who will kill him.

Greene's cantankerousness, his taste for the seedy, his sympathy for wise losers and weary cranks, all make him a confederate in the decadent camp. But above all it is his irreverence toward both church and state that grant him entry into a circle whose company, ironically, he would probably deplore. However, anyone who could create the diabolical Dr. Fischer of Geneva, the man famous for his "humble dinners" as well as his "bomb parties," knows a thing or two about supping with the devil.

The friendly feud between the Catholic priest and Communist mayor of *Monsignor Quixote* is similar in spirit to the conflict between the atheist and the fundamentalist who lock horns in Peter de Vries's *Slouching Towards Kalamazoo,* another comic novel with a serious center. Early in this story there is a highly imaginative scene in which the atheist and the fundamentalist debate religion in a public forum. By the end of the debate, the opponents have argued so convincingly that they have converted each other. But trading places, as it were, creates all kinds of social and domestic problems—including family swapping—problems that cannot be resolved until a rematch is held and the two men talk each other out of their conversions and back into their original positions. While Monsignor Quixote and his Communist friend may never reverse roles, they do find more common ground than one would think. Even to suggest such a dialogue would strike some as irreverent, not just to Catholicism but to communism as well. But Greene makes his point, and ultimately his brand of irreverence emerges as something closer to the spirit of the true devil's advocate.

In *Perfume,* Patrick Süskind is more of a devil's disciple than a devil's advocate. He is much bolder in his irreverent parody of religious ritual, in this case not just the ritual of crucifixion but also the ritual of the eucharist. Near the end of the novel there is an orgy so exaggerated, so obscenely comic, so absurdly horrible that it mocks prurience itself. The orgy is the result of a diabolical trick played on a crowd of spectators awaiting the execution of Jean-Baptiste Grenouille, the monster who has decimated the area's virgins in his pursuit of their scent. Unknown to these spectators, Grenouille has concocted an erotically stimulating perfume that he releases into the air as he ascends the scaffold where he is to be publicly dismembered.

The effect of this perfume as it wafts over the crowd is to unleash in the spectators their most primitive sexual instincts and arouse them to a passionate frenzy directed at the man they had come to see executed. They are filled with "naked, insatiable desire" and "driven to ecstasy." In a matter of minutes Grenouille changes from the vermin they cannot wait to exterminate into a creature of unimaginable beauty and perfection. To all assembled he becomes the embodiment of their deepest longings: the nuns see him as the Savior, the devil worshipers as Lucifer; he is the answer to every maiden's prayer and the image of masculinity every man idealizes.

In a grotesque parody of religious ecstasy, the spectators begin to perceive Grenouille as a sort of lubricous deity, able to see through them, to grasp them, to touch "their erotic core." They feel his hands upon them, not as hands that heal but as hands that fondle them in ways dreamed of only in their wildest fantasies.

After Jean-Baptiste Grenouille has appeared to the crowd assembled for his execution as an angel delivering them from the bondage of their inhibitions into the ecstasy of shameless sexual indulgence, he flees, knowing full well that once the people recover, they will turn against him as the agent responsible for their very willing debauchery. Knowing that the secret of his mastery of perfume is one that no one can ever understand or appreciate, he feels as estranged as any god whose message is beyond the comprehension of those it is intended to redeem. This is why he contrives to put himself at the mercy of the mob by anointing himself with a scent that will drive them to murder and cannibalism.

Once they have dismembered and devoured Grenouille, the "cannibals" are described as feeling delighted with themselves. Their very souls are animated, and there is a glow of innocence on their happy faces. Their reactions are clearly those of cultists or idolators whose spirits soar in frenzy and ecstasy once they have purged themselves of this uncontrollable desire to fulfill a mysterious ritual. They have participated in an unholy eucharist in which they have eaten the flesh and drunk the blood of a man to whom minutes before they had felt drawn as to some shining savior.

Interpreting Jean-Baptiste Grenouille as a parody of Christ may be taking decadent irreverence (and literary criticism) a bit far, but if Süskind is reminding us that we punish the wise along with the wicked, that, blessed or cursed, an eccentric is expendable, then his irreverence is less wicked than wise.

Since the word irreverence itself connotes disrespect for religious matters, it is not surprising that religion is the favorite target of decadent irreverence. However, anything society holds sacred is equally fair game, and decadents are just as eager to slaughter any of society's sacred cows. Motherhood has traditionally topped the list of the untouchables, but in *Travels with My Aunt* Graham Greene treats motherhood with less than filial piety. In the novel's opening scene, Greene turns the funeral of Henry Pulling's mother into high comedy when Henry accidentally presses the button that starts her casket on its irreversible slide into the flames.

Later, after Henry has placed the parcel containing his mother's ashes in an urn in the garden, "among the dahlias," the police arrive to confiscate the ashes, explaining to Henry that they have reason to suspect that the ashes are laced with cannabis. Almost apologetically Henry asks how they will be able to separate his mother from the marijuana without contaminating one or the other. The truth is that Henry doesn't know what to do with the ashes anyway and finds them something of an embarrassment. At the end of the novel, when it turns out that his flamboyant Aunt Augusta, a woman with a history of lovers of various castes and colors, is his real mother, the whole episode with the ashes becomes sublimely ridiculous.

Whereas Greene snickers at the sanctity of motherhood, Evelyn Waugh has fun mocking the stereotype of the concerned father. In *Brideshead Revisited,* Charles Ryder's father behaves as if his own son were almost a stranger. He has trouble remembering his son's age, always thinking Charles should be older than he is. When the two of them are obliged to have dinner together, Charles's father would rather read than talk. His son, a dutiful, intelligent young man is treated like an unwelcome guest his father would just as soon ignore. When Charles announces one day that he wants to study painting, his father thinks it a fine idea, especially if Charles can find an art school far from home, preferably somewhere out of the country.

Guy Huber in *Social Disease* is an equally dutiful son with parents who hardly know he exists. Guy is in his mid-twenties and very active in the New York club scene, but his father still sends him sixteenth birthday cards and, whenever he sees him, never fails to ask about how things are going at school. In fact, when Guy is arrested on vague charges brought against him by an

Arabian millionaire whose wives lust after Guy, Guy's father thinks it is some sort of prep school scrape and promises to write the dean assuring him that Guy will do better next term.

When Guy is sentenced to prison, he is sent to a minimum-security facility where, to his surprise, he runs into his father who is there "on some sort of tax evasion nonsense." The facility looks more like a fancy country club, and its inmates, whose crimes have mostly to do with embezzlement and fraud, are the very cream of society. In fact, the place is so posh that the fencing around it has been put there more to deter the curious than to detain the guilty. Guy's father enjoys the shishkebob and the rum punches, the massages and the theatricals, but to Guy the whole place is too tame, too much like his parents' parties—in a word, "too *Connecticut!*" However, he hangs on, and after a month his tennis game does improve.

Academe has long been a favorite target of satirists even though some may say that it is too easy a target. Be that as it may, it is also a teflon target to which nothing sticks. For years now writers like Evelyn Waugh (*Decline and Fall*), Kingsley Amis (*Lucky Jim*), Mary McCarthy (*The Groves of Academe*), Malcolm Bradbury (*The History Man*), and the outrageously irreverent Tom Sharpe (the *Wilt* books) have decked the halls with poison ivy, yet the institution remains impregnable. The reason for this is that few people outside the university (and not that many on the inside) understand how a university works or what really goes on there. Therefore, any fun made of it is bound to remain an "inside" joke, and the book is doomed to suffer the same fate as the works of those scholars who are the butt of the joke, scholars whose books, as one wag put it, are "widely read in narrow circles."

It is for this reason that David Lodge's brilliant academic satires are known almost exclusively among those they ridicule. In *Small World,* Lodge satirizes the life of the peripatetic professor who is forever going off somewhere to attend conferences that are more likely to be exercises in academic fraud and where the knowledge being pursued is more likely to be carnal. These high priests of Arcana are both defrocked and disrobed as Lodge exposes the wandering scholar who makes a profession of attending meetings around the world the way a pilgrim might move from shrine to shrine or a tourist from spa to spa. While decadence is invariably irreverent, it is important to remember that what is irreverent is not necessarily decadent. For this reason, not all writers who attack universities belong in the decadent camp. David Lodge, however, qualifies if only because his view of university life, were it not relieved by humor, would be hopelessly bleak. Decadents are very good at finding fault but not very good at finding solutions.

In the sixties and seventies, when Tom Wolfe was having a heyday taking pot shots at the hypocrisies of the counterculture movement, Hunter J. Thompson, one of the counterculture's very own, was just as busy taking pot shots at some of America's most hallowed shrines. In *Fear and Loathing in Las Vegas,* Thompson trains his guns on the town that many think defines decadence. It may seem strange, then, to call a book that lampoons Las Vegas decadent, or even irreverent, but anyone who has made a pilgrimage to that Mecca of Mammon and prayed to the goddess of luck in one of those cloistered casinos knows that it is safer to heckle a priest than it is to hassle a croupier. To introduce into this temple of greed a three-hundred-pound Samoan dressed in a fishnet T-shirt, a lawyer no less, who periodically retches down the side of a white Cadillac convertible, is to thumb your nose and look down it at the same time. Once Thompson finishes with Vegas, he is a candidate for one of the town's famous one-way bus tickets to the border.

But Thompson was less abused for *Fear and Loathing in Las Vegas* than he was for his scandalous inside look at what goes on beneath the bleachers at Churchill Downs in Louisville, Kentucky on Derby Day. In an article aptly titled "The Kentucky Derby is Decadent and Depraved," Thompson reveals a side of the derby never seen before. In fact, he never actually gets around to *seeing* the derby itself. He is too busy checking out the braggarts and the boozers, the loonies and the losers at what he calls this "jaded, atavistic freakout with nothing to recommend it except a very saleable 'tradition'" (175).

The time of the article is the early seventies, not long after the incident at Kent State, and when Thompson informs a loudmouth from Texas that a riot is expected at the derby (the Panthers plus busloads of white crazies) and that the cops, the National Guard, and twenty thousand troops from Fort Knox have been alerted, the Texan sobers up, throws up his hands, and says: "God Almighty! The Kentucky Derby! . . . "Why? Why *here*? Don't they respect *anything*?" (173)

Thompson admits that he and his companion didn't give a "hoot in hell" what was happening on the track. "We had come there to watch the *real* beasts perform," he says (178). Not only does Hunter watch, he reports, in graphic detail calculated to make him *persona non grata* in Kentucky for the rest of his life. Thompson's companion is an artist named Steadman who is there to sketch what no one would allow him to photograph. In particular Thompson is looking for a special kind of face, a face he has seen a thousand times at every Derby he has ever been to. "I saw it, in my head," he says, "as the mask of the whiskey gentry—a pretentious mix of booze, failed dreams and a terminal identity crisis; the inevitable result of too much inbreeding in a closed and ignorant culture" (179). Finally, after stealing two passes to gain admission to the derby, Thompson and Steadman spot the face they have been looking for. "Jesus, look at the corruption in the face!" Steadman whispers. "Look at the madness, the fear, the greed!" What Thompson sees is an old prep school classmate of his, now degenerated into a shady character with "fat slanted eyes and a pimp's smile," wearing a blue silk suit and boozing it up with friends who look like "crooked bank tellers on a binge" (183–184).

When Steadman then expresses a desire to see some Kentucky colonels but says that he does not know what they look like, Thompson tells him to "go back to the clubhouse men's rooms and look for men in white linen suits vomiting in the urinals" (184). So chaotic does the day become that the two men are unable to see the race, or even the track. Things get worse that night and the next day with Thompson and Steadman managing to alienate just about every Kentuckian they come in contact with. "Steadman was lucky to get out of Louisville without serious injuries," says Thompson, "and I was lucky to get out at all" (185).

Decadent irreverence tests the outer edges when it finds humor in situations that are ordinarily no laughing matter. At a time when starvation in third world countries is a social matter of grave concern to everyone from hyperactive rock stars to anorexic movie actresses, the fashion editor of *Glaze* magazine in Paul Rudnick's *Social Disease* sees it as an excuse for an innovative layout. If the magazine were to cover a famine, says Rudnick, its hype would be "Waistlines Are Back!" And when this same editor was told of man's first steps on the moon, she exclaimed, "Zero gravity. I see scarves!" Describing this editor as a woman who "relished all experience," Rudnick tells us that once she had even visited death row to shoot a fashion spread, "a layout she called 'Last Looks'" (109).

Rudnick also has fun with the sanctity of the work ethic, for there is no trace of it in Guy Huber. When told by his parents that he needs to find a job, Guy is "thoroughly shell-shocked . . . stunned, molested." His soul, says Rudnick, "hurtled beyond him, torn from his flesh." Although Guy may strike some as spoiled, Rudnick says that he is not "willfully spoiled." Rather he is spoiled "as a leaf is green, organically, tenderly. It had never occurred to him to hold a job" (51).

Surprisingly enough, Guy does land a job, the job his friends think he was born to hold: doorman at the "Club de." To celebrate the occasion, Guy wants to dress properly, and in recounting Guy's search for the perfect outfit, Rudnick has wicked fun with the sacrosanct history of poverty, sweatshops, and—holy of holies—the Great Depression. Guy prowls the second-hand stores until at last he happens upon the ideal costume: the same old tuxedo his very own grandfather had worn to a cotillion back in the halcyon days of F. Scott Fitzgerald. Guy is transported. He calls the tux "seraphic" and marvels that it is made of real wool and not dacron and polyester. Even more wonderful is the fact that the jacket is double-breasted with wide grosgrain lapels and that the pants are full and high-waisted with lots of pleats and sharp creases, the whole thing tapering to a perfect break at the ankle. To him the tux is nothing less than an engineering phenomenon with its "indestructible slouch" and "sweeping, almost Grecian contour," and he knows that it must have required as much time and material to make this one suit back then as it would take today to make hundreds of an inferior sort. "Tuxes like Guy's justify the Depression," says Rudnick; "the wracking poverty, the sweat-shop atrocity of the early rag trade are well honored" (89). Guy could not have enjoyed his tux more had he been told that starving coolies had hand-picked the wool from under the chins of milk-fed Mongolian sheep.

Even the dead are not spared Rudnick's irreverent wit. For example, there is a curious scene in *Social Disease* in which Licky, the gay friend of Venice and Guy Huber, has just announced to them that Tanzo, a mutual acquaintance, is a necrophiliac. Guy is stunned, but Licky assures him that if the corpse even twitches, "the date would be off." When Guy asks where Tanzo gets his bodies, Licky says the city morgue, where else? It's a madhouse most of the week, he adds, but "on Friday nights you can't get near the place" (38).

Perhaps the Biblical cynicism about letting the dead bury the dead makes the dead fair game. At any rate, they have no lobby, no activist group, no anti-defamation league to protect them. But the homeless do. Thus, this next remark of Licky's amounts to the "moral equivalent" of sticking out one's tongue at the starving: "The Homeless?" says Licky. "*Please.* What about the truly needy, the people without second homes? Where's *my* place at the beach?"

Decadents have always had a taste for the irreverent epigram that is based on an inversion of commonly accepted values. This is the legacy of Oscar Wilde who raised this sort of epigram to an art form. What makes it so appealing is its refreshing honesty. In an age of dreary self-help manuals where husbands are "supportive" and wives "get in touch with themselves" and children "learn to love themselves" and families "learn to communicate," there is a charming insouciance and a delightful cheekiness in a comment like this one of Paul Rudnick's: "A total lack of communication is the root of any happy family" (43).

Such insouciance is what makes many readers and not a few critics feel so uneasy about Tom Wolfe's *The Bonfire of the Vanities,* a wickedly wonderful book that spares no one. What bothers them about it is the fact that Wolfe dares to challenge the taboos of the day by exposing fraud and hypocrisy wherever he finds it, and where he finds it is often among groups that have become insulated from public scorn by virtue of their protected status as members of a minority or supporters of a cause against which no one may speak with impunity.

Wolfe's voice has been the most persistently irreverent one of the last few decades. With boldness and rare courage, Wolfe has had the audacity to ruffle the feathers of most of the age's protected species. From Black Panthers to social workers to civil rights activists, no group has escaped Wolfe's clear eye and common sense, regardless of that group's privileged status. His attack on hypocrisy wherever he finds it—and he finds it everywhere—is no different from Oscar Wilde's attack on the hypocrisy of his day. His acidly accurate dis-section of the New York art world in *The Painted Word* provoked the wrath of critics protective of their power to arbitrate artistic fashion according to whim and preference. His observation that, where most modern art is concerned, the picture exists to illustrate the text, infuriated those who resented, and de-lighted those who grasped, its essential truth.

He was no less a gadfly in his canny analysis of the proletarian roots of mod-ern architecture in *From Bauhaus to Our House.* To blame such untouchables as Walter Gropius and Mies van der Rohe for the ugliness of slablike buildings and the foolishness of flat roofs in wet climates was to some an unforgivable, to others an unsurpassable, affront. In an age in which Catherine Deneuve calls her perfume a costume, Tom Wolfe dares to ask the emperor whose scent he is wearing.

Tom Wolfe first took on the liberal establishment in the sixties with the publication of *Radical Chic,* a little book whose title has become a tag for fash-ionable support of trendy social causes. When *Radical Chic* first appeared, the question on everybody's lips was "How did Tom Wolfe get away with it?" Wolfe had been invited to attend a reception given by Leonard and Felicia Bernstein for some select leaders of the Black Panthers, a radical separatist protest faction determined to assert black power. The reception was given in the Bernsteins' swank east side apartment, complete with twin grand pianos, and while there Wolfe somehow managed to absorb like a sponge every nu-ance of that incredible affair. Some said he had a concealed tape recorder, oth-ers that he sat unobtrusively on the sidelines and scribbled notes. Still others credited him with total recall. Whatever the assumption (the truth is that he used shorthand), all wondered how he did it without being caught at it and getting thrown out on the spot.

Radical Chic is a carefully detailed, factually accurate "report" of an unimag-inable encounter between the racially dispossessed and New York's *haut monde*—or, as some put it at the time, between Black Rage and White Guilt. The image of Tom Wolfe mingling with that crowd, sampling canapés and sipping punch, and meanwhile taking it all in and writing it all down, calmly scribbling away while the innocent party-goers swirl around him, is the per-fect image of one breed of decadent writer—the person who is in the crowd but not of it. Proust was the first to mingle amiably among the fashionable and then to reveal their characters and their secrets in prose. Capote followed. Now Tom Wolfe is doing the same thing, and one wonders how long he is going to be able to get away with it.

Just as Wilde riled the Victorians, Tom Wolfe riles the neo-Victorians of the late twentieth century who, while they tolerate "nudity, violence, strong language, and sexual situations," do not tolerate unfavorable opinions about minorities (except WASPS), feminists, civil rights, affirmative action, and a host of other sacred cows about which dissent from the party line is tanta-mount to obloquy. In ridiculing such folly, Wolfe is as guilty as Wilde of offending the sensibilities of the age. One wonders what trials the twentieth century will dream up to silence its impious ingrates and merry malcontents.

Somerset Maugham once said that the modern way of silencing unpopular ideas is not the rack or the stake but the wisecrack. Fortunately, the decadent, with his wicked way with words, remains the master of it.

Chapter 4:

The Cult of the Self

I don't know why, but this glass refuses to flatter me!
Ronald Firbank, *The Flower Beneath the Foot*

Narcissism is at the very center of decadence. It is the magnetic core around which all other elements of decadence cluster. Wherever decadent elements appear in literature, they are invariably expressed through the refined sensibilities of an artist or a character for whom self-love is the ultimate love. Decadents are excessively preoccupied with their own emotions and the way they alone perceive the world. How they feel and what they think are of paramount importance to them—to the exclusion of any real interest at all in the feelings of others.

Other people exist primarily as mirrors in which decadents search for a flattering reflection of themselves. If they see praise or imitation, then they have found a fan—and maybe even a friend. Decadents obviously have little patience with "sheer plod" or "the common man" or "huddled masses yearning," and they certainly do not like to share the limelight with fellow egoists or suffer the pressure of each other's company unless it happens to provide them with an occasion for mutual ego bashing.

In his biography of Oscar Wilde, Richard Ellmann includes an exchange of telegrams between Wilde and James MacNeill Whistler. It is a perfect example of two decadent egos in three-quarter time—a veritable waltz of the wits:

Wilde: When you and I are together we never talk about anything except ourselves.

Whistler: No, no, Oscar, you forget. When you and I are together, we never talk about anything except me.

Wilde: It is true, Jimmy, we were talking about you, but I was thinking of myself.

"The narcissists," says Ellmann, "outdid each other" (271).

Decadent self-love runs the gamut from harmless vanity to overweening pride. Unfortunately, what often begins as a simple fondness for the looking glass may progress by way of a total preoccupation with oneself to a self-absorption so intense as to result in grandiose delusions. Dorian Gray begins by falling in love with his portrait. "I am in love with it, Basil," he says. "It is part of myself." And, since it and not he grows older and uglier, he ends up murdering Basil Hallward, the artist who painted the portrait, because Hallward has seen Dorian for what he really is. Age is anathema to Dorian. "When one loses one's good looks, one loses everything," he says. "When I find I am growing old, I shall kill myself." Ironically enough, this is precisely what he does when, in attempting to "kill" the portrait, he ends his own life.

In the meantime, "in a boyish mockery of Narcissus, he had kissed, or feigned to kiss, those painted lips. . . . Morning after morning he had sat before the portrait wondering at its beauty, almost enamoured of it" (258). And as the portrait continued to reflect his descent into irremediable corruption, "he would think of the ruin he had brought upon his soul, with a pity that was all the more poignant because it was purely selfish." Self-pity is the hand-maiden of self-love. After all, feeling sorry for oneself is something of a masochistic luxury, especially when the wounds are trivial and the suffering superficial.

As Dorian sinks more deeply into depravity, what began as mere vanity gives way to morbid pride. Often, returning home after days of debauchery, "he would sit in front of the picture, sometimes loathing it and himself, but filled, at other times, with that pride of individualism that is half the fascination of sin, and smiling with secret pleasure at that misshapen shadow that had to bear the burden that should have been his own" (298). And even after he has committed the heinous crime of murder, his mind is able to twist his transgressions into triumphs. "There were sins whose fascination was more in the memory than in the doing of them," he muses, "strange triumphs that gratified the pride more than the passions, and gave to the intellect a quickened sense of joy, greater than any joy they brought, or could ever bring, to the senses" (322). It is a chilling reminder of Dorian's callousness to see him, on the very evening of the day that he blackmails Alan Campbell into disposing of Hallward's body, happily attending a party given by a "very clever woman, with what Lord Henry used to describe as the remains of a really remarkable ugliness" (337).

Self-love can easily turn into self-hate, especially if the narcissist is petulant enough to blame his downfall on his beauty. Early in his iniquitous career, Dorian Gray receives a letter in which someone has written these flattering lines about him: "The world is changed because you are made of ivory and gold. The curves of your lips rewrite history." Later, when his life is beginning to turn sour, he remembers these lines, and suddenly he is filled with loathing for the author of such repulsive drivel and for himself for being its inspiration. In his fury he throws the mirror he has been gazing into on the floor and crushes it to splinters beneath his heel. "It was his beauty that had ruined him," he thinks to himself, "his beauty and the youth that he had prayed for" (387). Decadents are among the first to understand the punishment of answered prayers.

No one understood this merciless truth better perhaps than Truman Capote. *Answered Prayers* is the name he gave to the *magnus opus* that was to crown his career but which was left unfinished at the time of his death. According to his biographer, Gerald Clarke, Capote worked at the novel off and on for nearly twenty years, even published portions of it in magazines during that time, but he could not bring himself to finish it for a number of reasons, one of them being the fact that he wanted so much for the book to be a masterpiece that he frightened himself into literary paralysis. He was convinced that he was America's greatest living writer, and he deeply resented being overlooked by those who handed out Pulitzer Prizes and National Book Awards. Therefore, he was determined to "show them," but what he mainly ended up showing them was an enormous and self-destructive vanity.

This vanity so blinded him that he could not imagine the devastating effect the published portions of the novel were to have on those people on whom he had based his notorious characters. Thus, the novel that he hoped would earn him the highest accolades earned him instead the scorn of those who mattered most. Well written as the finished portions are, their popularity with the general public had more to do with their gossip value than with their literary value. And among those in this *roman à clef* whose identities were thinly disguised, there was the anger and hostility of the violated and the betrayed. Capote's ego had been stroked by the rich and powerful, and he had repaid them with disloyalty and what looked to them like nothing less than pure malice. To the bitter end, his ego blinded him to the cause of their resentment.

In the early stages of the obsession, the narcissist is only slightly more conceited than a teenager holding a comb in front of a plate glass window. If there is a mirror nearby, the narcissist will grace it with his reflection. Some of the literary treatments of this harmless affliction are little more than amusing fantasies. In Aubrey Beardsley's *Under the Hill,* for example, Tannhäuser is discovered at his morning ablutions "posturing elegantly before a long mirror, and [making] much of himself." After performing a few exercises in front of the mirror, "he would lie upon the floor with his back to the glass, and glance amorously over his shoulder." When the serving boys arrive to assist him with his bath, he delays a moment, standing "like Narcissus, gazing at his reflection in the still scented water, and then just ruffling its smooth surface with one foot, [steps] elegantly into the cool basin, and [swims] round it twice, very gracefully" (36).

In *The Flower Beneath the Foot,* Ronald Firbank describes a similar scene, this one featuring the novel's heroine, Laura de Nazianzi, as she prepares to retire for the night. She enjoys going to bed late, without anyone's help, because then one can, she thinks, "pirouette interestingly before the mirror in the last stages of deshabille, and do a thousand (and one) things besides that one might otherwise lack the courage for." In a wry footnote to this scene, Firbank lets us know that, years later, when Laura becomes Saint Laura, she writes in her *Confessions* that the recollection of doing this was always humiliating (48). In the same novel, the Hon. "Eddy" Monteith is insulted when he is mistaken for a cloakroom attendant: *"He* who had been assured he had the profile of a 'Rameses'!" He immediately locates a mirror and scans "with less perhaps than his habitual contentment, the high, liver-tinted hair, grey narrow eyes, hollow cheeks, and pale mouth like a broken moon" (94).

In *Decline and Fall,* Evelyn Waugh gives us a revealing glimpse of the sort of "bright young thing" that tiptoed through the twenties. When a party is given to celebrate the renovation of King's Thursday, once a venerable English country house but now a chrome and rubber horror, Waugh notes that "the first to come were the Hon. Miles Malpractice and David Lennox, the photographer, [who] emerged with little shrieks from an Edwardian electric brougham and made straight for the nearest looking glass" (171).

In "The Deluge at Norderney" Miss Malin Nat-og-Dag is also an egotist, as we have seen from the way she takes such enormous pride in her imaginary wickedness, but her egotism is fairly harmless. It is Count Augustus von Schimmelmann, who appears in both "The Roads Round Pisa" and "The Poet," whose egotism is destructive mainly because it is cloaked in deceit. Count Augustus is an enigmatic and elusive figure who spends a lot of time looking into mirrors to see what he is like. The difference between them is that Miss Malin's egotism, by advertising itself, loses its power to deceive whereas the Count dissembles behind a mask of benign indifference. In being what everyone wants him to be, he is satisfying the egotist's need to be admired. The irony is that because he is so wrapped up in himself, the self slips through his fingers and is lost. His wife is jealous because he is no longer *there,* even when he is with her, and one wonders if his chronic glancing into mirrors is not a way of reassuring himself that he really does still exist.

Such frivolous vanity, however, merely nourishes the extremes to which narcissism can be taken. More insidious is the temptation among decadents to exaggerate the importance of their responses and to believe that those responses, because they emanate from an extraordinary sensibility, have significantly more value than the responses of others. A decadent personality prizes its own wit, congratulates itself on its own cleverness, and is deeply impressed with its own accomplishments, no matter how trivial. This sort of personality lacks a sense of proportion, preferring, by the very nature of its abhorrence of the mob, those things which tend to be neglected to those things which are too easily praised. The decadent sees greater value in what society ignores than in what it honors, regardless of the circumstances.

Wilde composed a parable about Narcissus that brings Dorian's petulance and the illusions of all decadents into sharp focus. In this parable, Narcissus looks at his image in the water, but does not know that the water sees only its own image in his eyes. His portrait is truer than a mirror, for it reflects what is in his eyes—or behind his eyes, as it were—and that is the image of himself as he really is. As Wilde said in the preface to *Dorian Gray:* "It is the spectator, and not Life, that art really mirrors" (311–312).

In this statement Wilde is obviously not talking about identifying with a character or about becoming emotionally involved in the story. His point is that what readers see in a story is not objective reality but merely their own reflection, that readers turn all stories into their own, seeing only that which relates to themselves. However, while this may be true of readers in general, the decadent carries this propensity to self-congratulatory extremes. Huysmans declares that it is only natural that the decadent should prefer works that mirror his own personality while casually disregarding anything that does not. Des Esseintes, for example, has little respect for the "twaddle" of such literary giants as Voltaire or Rousseau or for the "moralizing inanities" of Diderot, preferring instead the "exponents of Christian oratory," men whose writings he favors in direct proportion to the obscurity of their names. Among more familiar names, however, he is strongly attracted to Pascal mostly because of his "austere pessimism" (148).

"But I just don't enjoy the pleasures other people enjoy!" he cries (211), echoing the neurotic narrator of Dostoyevsky's *Notes from Underground* who admits that he is worried by the discovery that there is no one like him and that he is unlike anyone else. "I am unique," he exclaims, "but they are all alike" (155). Where is the decadent to find his own reflection, then, but in the masochistic pleasures of works that speak to, as Huysmans puts it, "those deeper, deadlier, longer-lasting wounds that are inflicted by satiety, disillusion, and contempt upon souls tortured by the present, disgusted by the past, terrified and dismayed by the future"? (148) It was in this mood that Truman Capote was wont to go into seclusion for weeks at a time and reread every volume of Proust's *Remembrance of Things Past,* imagining himself hidden away in that famous cork-lined room, totally immersed in the private world of one of the century's most notorious narcissists. Capote modeled *Answered Prayers* on Proust's monumental work and identified with Proust whose ego became not just the center of the universe but the very universe itself.

Decadents despair of ever finding a kindred soul. Des Esseintes laments that he does not know anyone who is capable of appreciating the "delicacy of a phrase" or the "quintessence of an idea." He can find no one who understands even Mallarmé or Verlaine let alone the lesser-known poets and wonders where he should look to find a soul to match his own and a mind uncluttered by the commonplace, someone who values silence and who is much more comfortable with ingratitude and suspicion than with their doubtful opposites (213).

He sounds very much like Henry Higgins in *Pygmalion,* jealous of his solitude, happiest in his atmosphere of tomblike silence, secure in his taste, relieved at last to discover in a man like Pickering someone who can appreciate him without expecting that appreciation to be requited. It is a Holmes-Watson relationship made up of a combination of the greatest vanity reflected in the basest deference.

Like Des Esseintes, decadent readers are easily drawn to writers whom they find "all the more attractive and endearing by reason of the contempt in which they [are] held by a public incapable of understanding them" (185). Thus a reader so inclined would ordinarily eschew the routine best-seller in favor of a writer such as Thomas Pynchon or John Barth or Jorge Luis Borges—unless, of course, the best-seller happens to be by Stephen King or Sidney Sheldon, writers so distasteful to "educated" tastes that the decadent can take perverse delight in thumbing his nose at the literary establishment by wallowing in what it calls trash.

Decadents are likely to be drawn to minor writers whose very imperfections they find pleasing. Des Esseintes has a theory that a minor writer, a writer who is unpolished but individual, "distills a balm more irritant, more sudorific, more acid" than an author who is "truly great and truly perfect." In his opinion, it is in their confused efforts that you can find "the most exalted flights of sensibility, the most morbid caprices of psychology, the most extravagant aberrations of language called upon in vain to control and repress the effervescent salts of ideas and feelings" (185).

Both Truman Capote and Tennessee Williams, for example, have praised Jane Bowles's only novel, *Two Serious Ladies,* as possibly the best novel of the century. Capote, in fact, wrote the introduction to the small volume of Bowles's collected works (a novel, a play, and a handful of short stories), and it is as effusive as T.S. Eliot's excessive praise of Djuna Barnes in his introduction to a collection of her works.

In his definition of decadence, Clyde Ryals says that whereas the romantic "managed to keep his egotism subordinated in some measure to the ideals of romanticism, the decadent, on the contrary, always keeps the self in the foreground in his art; the self becomes the center of interest and the standard of value. Experience is valued for its own sake, the more varied the better. The decadent forgets that he is part of the universe and ignores his relationship to other forms of life. This in itself is decadence" (88). Joad maintains that it not so much his tendency to forget that he is part of the universe as to "misread his position in the universe" that marks a person as decadent. When he misreads his position, says Joad, the decadent is tempted to "take a view of his status and prospects more exalted than the facts warrant and to conduct his societies and to plan his future on the basis of this misreading" (15).

Joad could have Gide's *The Immoralist* in mind when he makes this cogent observation, for its hero, Michel, vows that once he has recovered from his bout with tuberculosis, he intends to discover "the authentic being," that real self that he identifies with the true Adam of the Old Testament, the Adam rejected by the Gospels. Michel is convinced that the spirit of the "old Adam" lives again within him in spite of the efforts of those around him, as well as his own former self, to suppress it. In order to uncover this spirit, Michel must peel away layers of acquired knowledge and cleanse himself of the cosmetic that conceals his true self, for he has already glimpsed the old Adam encrusted in husks just waiting to be stripped away.

He thinks of himself as a palimpsest and of his search for himself as the pursuit of the scholar who must peel away layer after layer before arriving at the original text. The thrill of the pursuit springs from the decadent fantasy that once these layers, like Salome's seven veils, are removed, once the palimpsest has been penetrated, what will emerge is some extraordinary being, maybe a prophet, maybe a superman, maybe, even, a god. Just after Jean-Baptiste Grenouille, in *Perfume,* has slain his ultimate victim, Süskind writes: "Feelings of humility and gratitude welled up within him. 'I thank you,' he said softly, 'I thank you, Jean-Baptiste Grenouille, for being what you are!' So touched was he by himself" (266).

Claude Ryals maintains that whereas the romantic placed his faith in hope, the decadent has replaced hope with *hubris*. "He does not cooperate with the moral machinery," says Ryals, "and he has neither hope nor consolation." The decadent, he says, seeks out experience for its own sake, as an end in itself and, therefore, he "cannot coordinate his experiences; he cannot order his own way" (91).

This description fits Michel who feels no need to "order his own way." It will happen, he assures himself, because it is destined to happen. He boasts that he no longer bothers to think at all or to waste time in self-examination. Convinced that he is guided by good luck and a benevolent destiny, he is afraid that looking too closely at what is happening to him might "profane the mystery" of the change that is slowly coming over him. Rather than interfere with the process, he is content to surrender to it, believing that whatever will be, will be. He remains on guard, however, against intrusions from previous indoctrination, and when he suspects that he is being influenced by his past education or his early moral indoctrination, he takes efforts to suppress that influence. He longs for perfection, and he thinks he can achieve it by dedicating his will to fortifying his body, to "turning it to bronze" (52–53).

The autobiographical novel has always been somewhat suspect among literary scholars who worry that even in the most skillful hands it becomes confessional, self-serving, and ultimately dishonest. In most cases self-pity vies with self-advertisement to create a hybrid sort of writing that shies away from that direct confrontation with life that only objectivity can recreate with any reasonable degree of verisimilitude. They will point out that the few successful autobiographical novels such as *Sons and Lovers, The Way of All Flesh,* and *Buddenbrooks* were written in the third person by authors who had been suddenly dislocated from the world they had taken for granted and forced to look back on their lives and see their lives whole, the scales having suddenly dropped from their eyes.

The decadent writer writes shamelessly of himself, convinced that his life is special enough to impress those who have either experienced less or been much less sensitive to their experiences. A recent example of this breed of egocentric literature is Michael Chabon's *The Mysteries of Pittsburgh,* a highly successful novel that caused considerable stir in the summer of 1988. That there is much to admire in this first novel by a young man in his early twenties must be admitted. The setting is memorably rendered, the atmosphere palpable, the mood sustained, the style mature. The novel is resonant with the ecstasy and torment of youth, the fantasies, the anguish, the poignant uncertainties of standing on the brink of life, unsure of your next step.

What ultimately gives *The Mysteries of Pittsburgh* its decadent tone, however, is the narcissism of its narrator, Art Bechstein. Art is sexually confused, torn between his love for a girl named Phlox and a friend named Arthur (his alter ego), and he is so immersed in the dilemma of his sexual ambivalence that he emerges as a character without a personality. We know less about him than we do about Phlox and Arthur or about his wild friend, Cleveland. The best we can glean is whatever seems to rub off on him from his friends: the impulsive sensuality of Phlox, the sophisticated sensuality of Arthur, the romantic self-destructiveness of Cleveland. In fact, the one he succumbs to and identifies with most closely for the most intense moments of the novel is Arthur, his alter ego. Art Bechstein, who is dark, looks in the mirror of Arthur Lecomte, who is fair, and sees a kind of idealized other self. In falling in love with Arthur, Art is really in love with himself.

At one point, early in the novel, Art admires Arthur's response to a tactless comment and says of his friend that he

stood straight, looked deeply, beautifully sympathetic for perhaps a tenth of a second, and nodded, with that fine, empty courtesy he seemed to show everyone. He had an effortless genius for manners; remarkable, perhaps, just because it was unique among people his age. It seemed to me that Arthur, with his old, strange courtliness, would triumph over any scene he chose to make; that in a world made miserable by frankness, his handsome condescension, his elitism, and his perfect lack of candor were fatal gifts, and I wanted to serve in his corps and to be socially graceful (31).

This is a perfect illustration of the decadent desire for the "fatal gifts" of the decadent ideal.

The most visible expression of the cult of the self is to be found in the artist who invents a personality for himself that then becomes his public persona and that helps him acquire a reputation that is often quite independent of his art. Sometimes the artist assumes the mask he has created for himself and ends up becoming his own most notorious invention. This is certainly true of Byron, with whom it could be said the tradition began, for the cult of personality is a romantic idea that was bound to arise once the artist had replaced the philosopher and the priest as the "unacknowledged legislators of the world," as Shelley proclaimed in *A Defence of Poetry.*

Oscar Wilde so immersed himself in the persona he had invented that he almost lost touch with the person he really was. "Would you like to know the great drama of my life?" he once asked. "It is that I have put my genius into my life—I have put only my talent into my works. I treated art as the supreme reality and life as a mere mode of fiction." The public Oscar Wilde was a figure that Wilde had been working on from his early days at Oxford, and it was well in place by the time he made his American tour in 1881–1882 when he was still not quite thirty years old. He was even being parodied for his posturing as an "aesthetic" in Gilbert and Sullivan's *Patience* before he had really accomplished anything of lasting importance. By the time he had established a literary reputation in the early 1890s, having written a best-selling novel and several extremely successful plays, he was already well known for his style of dress and talk. When his life fell apart in the mid-nineties and scandal sent him first to prison and then into exile, he was front-page news because he was already such a flamboyant public figure.

In this century, the public persona of F. Scott Fitzgerald is likely to come to mind when one thinks of the cult of personality. Here again was a writer who was—and still is—better known to many people for his reckless style of living than for his novels. He and Zelda made headlines as the jazz age's most colorful representatives. They were, as such personalities have come to be known, "celebrities." Ernest Hemingway might be said to have picked up where Fitzgerald left off. Although they were fellow expatriates in Paris in the twenties and contemporary writers of enormously popular novels, the figure of "Papa" Hemingway was an invention that gained momentum much later, during the second world war, and became a fixture in magazines and newspapers from then on until his death in 1961. Even today, people who have never opened a Hemingway novel have no trouble recognizing his grizzled face, just as they know of his macho reputation from rumor and hearsay.

Isak Dinesen may be the twentieth century's most intriguing example of the invention of public persona. In *Isak Dinesen and Karen Blixen: The Mask and the Reality,* Donald Hannah examines the difference between the private and public personae in detail. When she returned to Denmark from Africa at the age of forty-six, the woman who was to become famous as Isak Dinesen had been Baroness Karen Blixen-Finecke ever since her marriage to Bror Blixen-Finecke in 1914. When she chose the pseudonym Isak Dinesen, she combined her maiden name, Dinesen, with the Hebrew name Isak meaning "the one who laughs." But the name was much more than a pseudonym; it was the invention of a personality so enigmatic that reviewers of her first book, *Seven Gothic Tales,* knowing nothing at all of its author, had no clue to her identity. In her introduction to the first edition of the book, the most Dorothy Canfield Fisher could say was that its author "was not a Sicilian."

By adopting a pseudonym, Isak Dinesen had achieved the absolute anonymity that, at that time at least, she craved. She had set out against great odds to make a new life with a new start that included writing not only under a different name but also in English instead of her native language, Danish. It was as Isak Dinesen, then, that she established her reputation, only dropping the mask a bit after *Out of Africa* came out. But because we know that it, too, is, in a unique way, also a tale, we know that we do not get a realistic picture of Karen Blixen in it. Or, to put it another way, the picture we get of Karen Blixen, while not morally and aesthetically inaccurate, is a picture of her painted by her alter ego, Isak Dinesen.

Once her identity became known, the pseudonym became a persona. The Dinesen of the kohl-rimmed eyes and cloche hats, the Dinesen who weighed next to nothing and lived on oysters and champagne, the Dinesen who spoke with a husky, otherworldly voice as if she really were, as she was fond of saying, three thousand years old and had dined with Socrates, became the celebrity while Karen Blixen became a recluse. The best illustration of this division is to be found in the difference between the pastoral myth of *Out of Africa* and the bitter realities of drought and bankruptcy and heartbreak that are revealed in her *Letters from Africa,* published long after her death.

What separates Dinesen's public persona from the personae of Wilde or Fitzgerald or Truman Capote is the fact that, at least in the beginning, the artist and the celebrity were one and the same: Isak Dinesen. No one knew of the existence of Karen Blixen until *Out of Africa* appeared. Later, however, once she became well known, her ardent admirers thrust celebrity status on her and encouraged her to play the role she had discovered she could play so well. Like Marilyn Monroe and Elvis Presley, she succumbed to the temptation to be what her fans wanted her to be, except that her age and her health—and, one would like to think, her wisdom—prevented her from going too far. Hannah thinks that Dinesen assumed a mask "in order to fill the emptiness she found in her environment in Denmark" and that she "created an artistic conception of herself to replace the identity of which circumstances had robbed her" (52). Elsewhere he speaks of the feeling she had of living in a vacuum. When a persona is created to fill a void, it is almost inevitable that the mask will take over. Today in Europe, Karen Blixen is the artist; Isak Dinesen is the mask.

If religion is the opiate of the people and Marxism the opiate of the intellectual, then narcissism is the opiate of the decadent. The "me-ism" of the 1970s simply told him that everybody was now doing what he had been doing all along, quite naturally. Whether out of self-consciousness, self-righteousness, or self-love, mirror-gazing has become the number one spectator sport of the age. Unfortunately, for decadents more so than for others, looking into a mirror may all too easily come to resemble Dorian Gray confronting the ugliness of his portrait or Dr. Jekyll facing the horror of Mr. Hyde.

Chapter 5:

A Vast Carelessness

Is the world to go to pot, or am I to go without my tea? I say that the world may go to pot for me so long as I always get my tea.
Dostoyevsky, *Notes from Underground*

Irresponsibility is the offspring of selfishness, and decadents have a well-deserved, if somewhat inflated, reputation for putting their needs first. What makes their brand of selfishness seem more blatant than the selfishness of society in general is that decadents do not hide behind what they consider to be a façade of self-righteousness. They do not excuse self-interest in the name of security or sacrifice or reward by employing rationalizations such as "My family comes first," "My children come first," "I earned it," "I deserve it," "I'm worth it." They see their selfishness as merely a reflection of society's own. What they forget is that blaming society's selfishness for their own is itself a rationalization, one that leads, as rationalizations always do, to excesses that are destructive to both deceived and deceiver.

Decadent irresponsibility begins where decadent irreverence leaves off. Whereas irreverence is mostly passive and harmless, irresponsibility is active and ultimately destructive. Irreverence is idea, irresponsiblity is deed. When that idea becomes impulse and that impulse turns into action, somebody is bound to get hurt.

At its most benign, decadent irresponsibility takes the form of what Joad in *Decadence* calls a "Laodicean indifference." In a world not renowned for justice or fairness or virtue, a world that daily teaches lessons in indifference to suffering, to sacrifice, to the rights and feelings of others, an attitude of "benign neglect" is, to the decadent personality, almost a matter of good manners. As Joad points out, a live-and-let-live attitude ought to contribute, one would think, to social agreeableness, yet such tolerance is quite often looked upon as a sign of decadence, probably because it looks less like active tolerance than like passive indifference. Even so, given the history of persecution, Joad asks, "can there be tolerance without indifference?" (77)

"I am periodically accused of being 'decadent,'" Isak Dinesen told Daniel Gillès the summer before she died. "That is no doubt true, as I am not interested in social questions, nor in Freudian psychology. But," she added, "the narrator of the *Thousand and One Nights* also neglected social questions, and it is also no doubt for that reason that today the Arabs still gather in their public squares to hear her stories. As for me I have one ambition only: to invent stories, very beautiful stories" (Thurman, 265).

An equally candid expression of indifference toward the world and its problems was expressed by Truman Capote in an interview with Denis Brian. When Brian asked him what subject he would like to take up if he could communicate with the world on international television, Capote replied that his mind simply did not work that way. "If I said I wanted to talk of the need for peace, I'd be a hypocrite," he said, "because I don't care about it." In fact, he added, "there's no subject I could imagine talking about to an international audience, to try to convince them, that I wouldn't feel hypocritical about." Not content to leave it at that, the interviewer pressed Capote, asking him what he would want changed if he could appear before people who had the power to effect change. "For example, pollution might particularly concern you," he suggested. "But it doesn't, you see," Capote insisted. "I really, truly don't *care* enough about any of these subjects to get up and talk about them." Undeterred, the interviewer hammered away, until he finally got Capote to admit that, if he had a family, he guessed he would want them to be provided for in the event of his death. "I don't feel *totally* disconnected," he concluded lamely (*Conversations*, 230–231).

If there is no tolerance without indifference, then indifference becomes something of a virtue. What concerns Joad is that indifference derives not from tolerance but from skepticism. Only when one's own beliefs are uncertain can one be tolerant of the beliefs of others, for where doubt exists there is little risk of conflict. In short, one tolerates when one does not care. Joad notes that skepticism increases in an age of "growing material prosperity and diminishing spiritual intensity" and feels that such an age qualifies for the title of decadent because the skepticism it encourages leads to the kind of irresponsibility that takes the form of indifference.

While it is tempting to apply this assessment to the last half of the twentieth century, it must be done with caution. On the one hand, it is true that in the time since Joad's book came out at the end of the second world war, there has been an unprecedented increase in material prosperity. On the other hand, however, whether or not there has been an accompanying decline in spiritual intensity is less clear and much more difficult to gauge. There seems to have been a noticeable resurgence of religious enthusiasm within the last decade or two, but religious enthusiasm is not quite the same thing as spiritual intensity. The eighteenth-century rationalists had spiritual intensity, as did the free-thinking social reformers of the Victorian era. Whatever the measure of intensity of contemporary religious ardor may be, there is good reason to believe that it does not accurately characterize the age or do very much after all to mitigate a pervasive skepticism of the sort that creates the climate of indifference and irresponsibility to which Joad refers and in which decadence flourishes.

Such a climate did exist at the end of the nineteenth century when the material comforts of the gilded age had cooled the ardor of the reformers. Not by any means did all or even most people share this affluence or, for that matter, the skepticism that comes when pampered bodies take precedence over anguished souls. But those who were fortunate enough to enjoy the prosperity of the times set the tone for the age, and foremost among them were the decadents who, by both copying and mocking the carelessness of the privileged, managed to have the best of both worlds. At one point in *Dorian Gray* Basil Hallward says to Lord Henry Wotton, "You like everyone; that is to say, you are indifferent to everyone" (148). Decadent irresponsibility in its most agreeable form is precisely this friendly indifference to the attention the world insists on drawing to itself.

Art historian Arnold Hauser equates this attitude with the French concept of the dandy, the figure Oscar Wilde was emulating when he considered his own life his superior work of art and the figure Baudelaire places above the artist because he represents the ideal of an "absolutely useless, purposeless, and unmotivated existence" (*Social*, 905). "The elegance of dress, the fastidiousness of manners, the mental austerity, are," to Baudelaire, "only the external discipline which the members of this higher order impose upon themselves in the commonplace world of today; what really matters is the inward superiority and independence, the practical aimlessness and disinterestedness of life and action" (904). Susan Sontag calls such detachment the prerogative of the elite and points out that the dandy was the nineteenth century's "surrogate for the aristocrat in matters of culture." Dandyism today, she argues, is what has come to be known as "camp," a modern sensibility that answers the problem of how one can be a dandy in the age of mass culture (*Against,* 288).

The decadent treats all alike; he cannot be bothered to make distinctions. In *Pygmalion* Henry Higgins announces that the only social distinction he makes is to treat flower girls like duchesses and duchesses like flower girls. He cares nothing about the feelings on either side, as can be seen in the way his "royal" treatment of the flower girl, Eliza Doolittle, causes her considerable grief. Higgins is not intentionally unkind, but the line between not noticing and not caring is a fine one, and his insensitivity to the line causes thoughtless indifference to turn into thoughtless cruelty. The decadent's narrow vision can easily blind him to honest need and genuine suffering. In fact, this very blindness can often make things worse than they were.

Lord Henry's indifference blinds him to the consequences of his influence on Dorian and thus to the suffering Dorian is causing others, particularly Basil Hallward. Right up to the end Lord Henry continues to give irresponsible advice to a Dorian who is, at that point, clearly troubled by what is happening to him. Lord Henry misses the point when Dorian upbraids him about having lent Dorian a copy of *Against Nature* and begs him never to lend that book to anyone else. "It does harm," he cries. Instead of seeing this as a call for help, Lord Henry cannot resist the temptation to be flippant. "My dear boy," he says, "you are really beginning to moralize. You will soon be going about like the converted, and the revivalist, warning people against all the sins of which you have grown tired" (385). He then launches into a speech on the sterility of art and its inability to influence action. Dorian knows better, but it is too late. In the next chapter Dorian is dead, and we can only hope that Lord Henry was not asked to speak at the funeral.

No one is more protective of her own feelings or indifferent to the feelings of others than Mrs. Gareth in *The Spoils of Poynton*. It is a decadent trait to prefer things to people, and Mrs. Gareth demonstrates this in her utter disregard for anything but her precious furnishings. Her son's happiness means nothing to her, and she will stop at nothing to keep him from having the woman he loves if it means maintaining control over the furnishings. The hairsplitting scruples of her young companion, Fleda Vetch, may in fact be nothing but cunning machinations, but Fleda is still caught in Mrs. Gareth's clutches, mere bait in the trap to ensnare Owen and get back Poynton and the spoils that mean everything to her.

Whereas Mrs. Gareth is obsessed with furniture, the governess in James's *The Turn of the Screw* is obsessed with evil and determined to root it out no matter what the cost to Flora and Miles, the children she feels it is her duty to save. Ironically, responsibility in her case turns into irresponsibility. She upsets the household and puts the children's lives in jeopardy in her zeal to exorcise demons which she claims possess the children but which, it would seem, actually possess her. On the surface, at least, it looks as if it is the governess herself, not the late Miss Jessel or Peter Quint, who finally drives Flora to hysteria and Miles to his death. In spite of the intriguing ambiguity of the story, one thing is clear: the governess seems blissfully unaware of the fact that by pampering her own delusions she is putting her charges in harm's way.

Unlike the governess in *The Turn of the Screw* who does harm out of a sense of misguided charity, Cazotte, the crafty artist in Isak Dinesen's *Ehrengard,* is quite deliberate in his intention to cause trouble. Cazotte, a portrait painter and notorious seducer, plots to shame Ehrengard, the stalwart virgin who guards the newborn prince of the house of Fugger-Babenhausen. Cazotte's intention is to effect an "emotional" seduction of Ehrengard, and the way he intends to accomplish his plan is to embarrass her in public and cause her to blush. By blush, he means no ordinary blush, but the sort of blush that rivals the *Alpen-Glühen,* that roseate tint that colors a snow-covered mountainside just at sunrise. When he accidentally discovers that Ehrengard takes a bath every morning in a nearby lake, Cazotte decides to hide in the woods at the edge of the lake and paint her portrait, without her knowledge. His plan is to unveil the portrait at a palace exhibition at which Ehrengard will be present, and in taking her by surprise, to cause her to experience an irresistible and overwhelming blush over her entire body. He obviously cares nothing about her feelings in his selfish and insensitive attempt to embarrass her, to seduce her emotionally just to satisfy his own peculiar lusts.

In Gide's *The Immoralist,* Michel displays a similarly callous indifference, first to his wife, and later to his workers. Early in the story, Michel is the one with tuberculosis, the one who must be coddled and nursed and consoled. Later, when he recovers and his wife becomes ill with the same disease, Michel uses her illness as an excuse to pursue his newly discovered sensual pleasures. As her body is wracked with illness, his is restored to vigorous health, and he takes great delight in developing it and tanning it and admiring it.

As their roles reverse and Michel is increasingly tempted to live a double life, he discovers not only the necessity but also the pleasure of deception. "My very dissimulation increased my love," he says. It creates a peculiar bond between them. Deception, like love, requires a partner; the difference is that where deception is involved, the deceiver is in complete control of the situation, and his success depends on secrecy. If he is found out, the deception dissolves and with it the pleasure. "Perhaps this need to lie cost me something, at first," he admits, "but I soon realized that what are supposedly the worst things (lying, to mention only one) are hard to do only when you have never done them; but that each of them becomes, and so quickly! easy, pleasant, sweet in the repetition, and soon a second nature" (60). It was Lord Henry Wotton in *Dorian Gray* who said that "the sin we had done once, and with loathing, we would do many times, and with joy" (205). This is certainly the case with Michel, for he boasts of the fact that once he had overcome an initial disgust, he ended up "enjoying the dissimulation itself, savoring it." He feels that his life is becoming richer and fuller, and that he is advancing toward a "more delicious happiness" (60), a happiness gained at the expense of his responsibility to Marceline as her husband and guardian.

Later, when Michel turns to poaching from his own land, he is unconcerned about the fact that innocent laborers might be blamed for his crimes or that their forced compliance might ultimately corrupt them. With his newfound health comes self-gratification with no regard for the welfare of others. In fact, the way he first takes to poaching from himself involves blackmailing a workman he catches at it into teaching Michel how to poach. "With what passion I continued poaching!" he admits (131), blithely indifferent to the fact that he has turned an ordinary poacher (poaching, after all, is a time-honored crime) into a depraved conspirator.

By contrast, Gustav Aschenbach in Thomas Mann's *Death in Venice,* becomes increasingly self-centered the more the cholera infects his body and his health deteriorates. In Michel's case, disease had caused him to be preoccupied with the healthiness of his body whereas Aschenbach ignores the growing threat of the cholera epidemic and becomes increasingly careless about his own health and finally his own life. At one point he relishes luscious overripe strawberries of the sort that no cautious person would dare touch, especially in a time of cholera. But Aschenbach actually seems to welcome the disease, seemingly as a corollary to the fever that has been inflaming his emotions. He becomes ridiculously vain, to the point of allowing a Venetian barber to dye his hair and rouge his cheeks in a grotesque attempt to look younger and more attractive. Aschenbach's vanity is, of course, pure delusion, part of the whole web of deception in which his mind and emotions have been ensnared.

His vanity, his deceptiveness, his irresponsibility have all been nurtured by his passion for solitude. He chooses to spend a lifetime in what amounts to creative solitary confinement because he believes that "solitude gives birth to the original in us, to beauty unfamiliar and perilous—to poetry." What Aschenbach does not realize, until it is too late, is that, as Mann says, solitude also gives birth to the opposite, "to the perverse, the illicit, the absurd" (456). This has been the fate of most hermits in decadent literature from Des Esseintes in *Against Nature* to Jean-Baptiste Grenouille in *Perfume*. Solitude turns them into morally irresponsible monsters who, no longer able to engage in the wholesome interaction of the social dialectic, destroy themselves in a futile attempt to reconcile the irreconcilable opposites in their own natures.

Particularly irresponsible is Aschenbach's total disregard for the welfare of Tadzio and his family. Because news of the cholera has appeared only in the German-language newspapers among those available to foreign tourists, Tadzio's family is unaware of the danger. Aschenbach knows that a word of warning from him would send them packing and probably save their lives, but he cannot bear the thought of losing Tadzio. Even worse, he gets a curious pleasure out of keeping this secret and watching the family go about in ignorance as the threat increases. It matters little in the case of Tadzio anyway, he thinks, since he notices that the boy's teeth, which are jagged and bluish and unhealthy looking, indicate that he is delicate and sickly and not likely to live long. Aschenbach, says Mann, "did not try to account for the pleasure the idea gave him" (465).

Aschenbach even finds the idea of secrecy itself morbidly pleasing. "The knowledge that he shared the city's secret, the city's guilt—it put him beside himself, intoxicated him. . . . His thoughts dwelt upon the image of the desolate and calamitous city, and he was giddy with fugitive, mad, unreasoning hopes and visions of a monstrous sweetness." For a moment he toys with the idea of warning Tadzio's family and then nobly departing, but a moment later he scorns that sentiment in favor of "the boons that chaos might confer" (491).

Irresponsibility towards oneself is a curious counterpart to decadent hedon-

ism in which the insistent voice of one's own desires is one's only acknowledged responsibility. Whether the motivation is self-love or self-loathing, the
focal point is the self and its needs regardless of the consequences. One of
Mann's recurring themes is the curious way in which irresponsibility can turn
against its host and destroy him. Next to Aschenbach, the most famous example in Mann's works of this curious self-destructiveness is Hans Castorp in *The
Magic Mountain.* Castorp is a healthy young man who travels to Switzerland to
visit a friend in a tuberculosis sanitorium and becomes so enamoured of the
life of the invalid that he feigns illness until he finally contracts the disease
and is able to play the part legitimately. There is a world of difference between
the saint, who sacrifices his health in the service of others, and the decadent,
whose sacrifice is a voluptuous form of suicide in which he becomes a gloat-
ing accomplice to the disease that is ravaging his body.

When the victim is oneself, the irresponsibility seems less objectionable because it is felt that others are spared. However, others can and frequently do
suffer vicariously, especially those who either care about or must care for the
one whose indifference to his own welfare may have made him dependent on
them. Literature is full of characters who crave so much attention that they
will deliberately put themselves in a position to be pampered as a way of manipulating others. Sick or not, they will be in control, and no one has more
power with fewer constraints than the demanding sick person who has found
a slave to nurse him.

The desire to manipulate others is the most insidious expression of decadent
irresponsibility, and it usually manifests itself in behavior that is much more
aggressive than the relatively passive possessiveness of a tyrannical patient.
Des Esseintes, for example, takes great delight in corrupting a poor young boy
he finds on the streets by treating him to the good life and then abandoning
him to what he imagines will be a life of crime. The way he goes about this is
to take the boy to a brothel where he arranges with the madam for the boy to
enjoy six weeks of carnal delights. At the end of this period, the boy is to be
left on his own to find the money to support his habit any way he can. Des
Esseintes is convinced that the boy will have become so accustomed to the expensive pleasures Des Esseintes has subsidized that he will undoubtedly pursue
a life of crime in order to continue paying for that life. Even though Des
Esseintes never finds out for sure what happens to the boy, the thought of the
boy's inevitable corruption gives him a curious thrill. For a long time he
checks the newspapers daily for an account of the murder he is sure the boy
will commit in order to obtain the money he needs to support his addiction.

While we never know what happens to Des Esseintes's young victim, we do
know what happens to the young victim of Cipolla, the diabolical magician
who plays an obscene trick on Mario in Thomas Mann's "Mario and the Magician." Cipolla is a deformed and grotesquely made up hypnotist who swears
that he can get people to do anything he wants them to do, even against their

will. He is true to his word when, during an evening-long performance, he breaks down even the most stubborn resistance and gets ordinarily staid people to do the most ridiculous things. Most unsettling of all, however, is his affront to Mario, a young waiter who does not want to be made a fool of the way Cipolla has disgraced the other young men by turning them into dancers who twitch and wriggle on the stage like puppets. But Mario does finally succumb, and his disgrace is made all the more humiliating when Cipolla, pretending to be Mario's girlfriend, gets Mario to kiss his repulsive face. Cipolla is delighted with his success, but Mario, once the spell is broken, pulls a gun and shoots the magician.

Mario's weakness is that he is unable to counter Cipolla's hypnotic powers with positive resistance. Like most who try to resist hypnosis, he can only think negatively, telling himself that he will not allow himself to be hypnotized, instead of combatting hypnosis by concentrating on something else. Mann's point is that "not willing is not a practicable state of mind: *not* to want to do something may be in the long run a mental content impossible to subsist on" (251). "Between not willing a certain thing and not willing at all—in other words, yielding to another person's will—there may lie too small a space for the idea of freedom to squeeze into" (251–252). While decadents who manipulate others may behave like Cipolla, the magician, they can just as easily become like Mario and surrender to a mesmerizing influence, a disturbing side of the decadent personality that will be taken up later.

Hulga Hopewell, in Flannery O'Connor's "Good Country People," is equally defenseless against the machinations of Manley Poynter, a young man posing as a Bible salesman, who delights in taking advantage of the weaknesses of others. In Hulga he spots the weakness the moment he sees through her façade of nihilism. It is an interesting encounter in terms of decadence, for in this story the main characters are both guilty of the two extremes of irresponsibility common to the decadent temper. In Hulga's case, it is the irresponsibility born of an intellectually acquired belief in nothing. Hulga is homely, hulking, and slatternly, with a Ph.D. in philosophy, a wooden leg, and the arrogance of the ugly intellectual. Because she has a very low opinion of herself, she has changed her name from Joy to Hulga and found comfort in a philosophy of nihilism.

Manley Poynter, on the other hand, is uneducated but worldly-wise. Because his nihilism comes naturally to him, it easily overpowers Hulga's, for hers is an attitude she has adopted, an attitude which is little more than a pose. She is able to behave irresponsibly because she depends unthinkingly on the positive values of "good country people" to sustain her. She can break the rules because she thinks she can count on others to follow them. It comes as a great shock to her to find herself outfoxed by Manley Poynter who has lured her to the loft of a barn and talked her into removing her wooden leg. When he takes it and will not give it back, she appeals to him as a Christian and as "good country people" to return it to her, but he refuses. He then confesses

that he is not a Bible salesman, not a Christian, and certainly not "good country people." He also tells her that he believes in absolutely nothing, that he has
always believed in absolutely nothing, and that his nihilism is the real thing.
At that point he grabs her leg and leaves her to get down from the loft as best
she can.

Hulga and Manley are similar to Mario and Cipolla in the way that both
couples reflect opposite poles of decadent irresponsibility. Like Cipolla,
Manley is the decadent manipulator while Hulga, like Mario, displays decadent gullibility in the way she lets herself be manipulated because she thinks,
until it is too late, that she is in control. In both stories, however, the characters who exploit the weaknesses of others out of a total disregard for their
well-being are the ones who are guilty of the heedless sort of selfishness that
results in careless cruelty.

Sometimes decadent irresponsibility expresses itself in what its perpetrators
see as a well-intentioned desire to intervene in others' lives, to manipulate
their destinies, to play Pygmalion. The Pygmalion syndrome became a concept in the 1890s with the publication of *Trilby* by George du Maurier. In this
novel, a Hungarian musician named Svengali takes complete control of the career of Trilby O'Ferrall, an artist's model whom he turns into a great singer.
The novel is hardly read anymore, but the name Svengali is still used to describe anyone who maintains a mesmerizing influence over someone else.
George Bernard Shaw captured this syndrome perfectly in the character of
Henry Higgins in his play aptly called *Pygmalion*. One side of Higgins is the
recluse who desires nothing more than to be left alone to pursue his linguistic
studies undisturbed. The other side is the manipulator who jumps at the
chance to turn a flower girl into a duchess and pull a fast one on the society for
which he feels only contempt.

The Pygmalion syndrome is also apparent in the character of Elliott
Templeton, the archetypal snob in Somerset Maugham's *The Razor's Edge*.
Manipulation, of course, is a form of snobbery since it arises from a conviction
that one knows better what others should do than they do themselves. Elliott,
a wealthy American expatriate, tries his best to take young Larry Darrel in
hand when Larry moves to Paris to "think things out," but Larry will have
none of it. Elliott wants to introduce Larry to the right people, the right
restaurants, the right tailors while Larry is happy keeping to himself and
spending his days reading philosophy. Once Elliott realizes the futility of his
endeavors, he throws up his hands and drops Larry in disgust. Templeton has
more luck with his niece, Isabel, and her family after they lose everything in
the 1929 stock market crash and become dependent on him. He fusses over
everything from house furnishings to wines to the proper couturiers for
Isabel.

In real life, such manipulation often takes odd turns. The relationship between Oscar Wilde and Lord Alfred Douglas was a contest between two ex-

perienced manipulators vying for control over each other. And Wilde, as we
have seen, had a profound and deliberate influence on André Gide during
Gide's formative years. During his lifetime, Truman Capote tried on several
occasions to take over the lives of others. Although he did succeed in manipulating the careers of Joanna Carson and Lee Radziwill, he never succeeded in
turning them into the successes he had assured them would be theirs. His plan
to rescue Joanna Carson from the shadow of her famous husband hardly got
off the ground before she backed away but still managed to remain his friend.
Such, however, was not the case with Lee Radziwill, the jealous sister of
Jacqueline Kennedy Onassis. He convinced her that she would be an actress of
stature and a star, but the parts he arranged for her to play only publicized her
appalling lack of talent. When he compounded this humiliation by betraying
her confidences, she turned on him with a vengeance. While it lasted, however, Capote was wildly enthusiastic. According to his biographer, Gerald
Clarke, "Never before had he had either the time or the opportunity to play
Pygmalion on such a grand scale" (384). It was Capote's dream, he says, to
shape Lee Radziwill's future, "to make of her life a work of art. He saw her
not merely as a character in a novel," he adds, "but as a character in *his* novel"
(385).

The most notorious example of the Pygmalion syndrome in real life has to
be the four-year relationship between Isak Dinesen and her protégé, the
young Danish poet, Thorkild Bjørnvig, a relationship they referred to as
their "pact." In 1974 Bjørnvig published an account of this relationship in a
book entitled *The Pact* in which he tells how in the early fifties he came
under the spell of Dinesen who, at sixty-four, was twice his age at the time
their sexless "affair" began. It was sexless because of the syphilis she had con-
tracted from her husband in Africa shortly after their marriage in 1914, but
in every other respect it was a close communion between a strong-willed
woman who wanted to mold a young man to her measure and a young man
willing to be molded.

The fact that Bjørnvig was married and a father did not deter Dinesen from
trying to manipulate his life the way she had tried before to manipulate the
lives of others, attempts that always ended in failure. Dinesen made it clear
that she considered their pact to be "a mystical union, a vow of eternal love, a
covenant similar to the covenants she had felt between herself and Wilhelm
[her father], Farah [her servant on the farm], and the Africans" (Thurman,
335). According to Judith Thurman in her biography of Dinesen, "there was
a rather more disturbing, grandiose dimension to it: Bjørnvig was, as
[Dinesen] saw it, entrusting his soul to her, in exchange for her eternal vigi-
lance and protection" (335). Dinesen had long been fond of claiming that she
had promised her own soul to the devil in exchange for the gift of telling
tales, and now, says Thurman, "she took over the demonic role and promised
the same gift of genius to someone else" (335).

Over their four-year relationship, Dinesen interfered so thoroughly in

Bjørnvig's life that his health deteriorated and his marriage came close to collapse. At one point, just before he was about to leave for Bonn to study there, Dinesen made him sign a document which she called "The Ritual of Choice" in which he renounced all doubt or regret concerning his decision and agreed that he accepted the pact of his own free will. He also introduced her to a decadent young man he thought might act as his surrogate while he was away. The young man was Jørgen Gustava Brandt, a nineteen-year-old poet and dandy "in the English manner" whom Judith Thurman describes as "a cynic of the darkest hue, a jester, and a desperado." He was an incorrigible gossip, something Dinesen loved, but it was also true that "nothing was safe from his mockery," not even Dinesen herself (353).

Even though Dinesen is the one who had arranged for Bjørnvig to study abroad, it was not long before she schemed to get him back to Denmark, and once she had him back, she even managed to get him to stay at her home, Rungstedlund, for extended periods of time at the extreme displeasure of his wife. Later, when Dinesen found out that he was having an affair with a woman she knew, she turned nasty and mocked the lovers mercilessly, even though at one time she had encouraged him to do such a thing. Part of her anger, however, had to do with his refusal to participate in a "blood pact." She called him a coward, but at that point, he was seeing clearly how out of hand this whole business was getting. At the outset she had warned him that she feared she might succumb to megalomania and had asked him to promise to tell her if he saw signs. By the time the pact was dissolved, it was clear that her fears had been well founded.

Bjørnvig survived the effects of this strange pact by putting his domestic life back together and returning to his poetry. Dinesen had already seen the break coming and was prepared to deal with it in the only way she knew how, by writing stories. It is the ironic fate of the artist that it is art that first stimulates emotional excess and art that finally stems it. The tales Dinesen wrote during this period are among her finest. Two of them have to do with the attempts of one person to exercise complete power over another, and one of them is a particularly imaginative expression of something she had known all along, try as she might to deny it: that art cannot be transformed into life. Life and art remained for her the blessed opposites that held the key to each other, and there would always be a line between them. In "The Immortal Story" (*Anecdotes of Destiny*) a rich old man named Mr. Clay hears a story he wants to see re-enacted in real life, and he goes to great trouble and expense to arrange it, but he very quickly loses control of the characters and their actions. Dinesen had first dealt with this theme in "The Poet," the last of the *Seven Gothic Tales*. But the theme has its most personal expression in terms of Dinesen herself in "Echoes" (*Last Tales*), a story in which her fictional counterpart, Pellegrina Leoni, tries to remake others in her own image and fails. Ole Wivel, a long-time friend of hers, once said that Dinesen "suffered from a craving for power" and that she "toyed with human fates in spite of her contempt for such toying. . . . She was a paradox," he said, "outside of any moral category—and also," he added, "a bad judge" (*Romance,* 216). Such is the destiny of the decadent temperament.

Charles Strickland, in Somerset Maugham's *The Moon and Sixpence,* is an artist who is remorseless in his manipulation of others to satisfy his own mad ambition. When he can no longer contain his desire for independence and artistic freedom, he abandons his wife and family as well as his job as a stockbroker to go off on his own and paint. Along the way he steals another man's wife, then drives her to suicide, after which, without an ounce of remorse, he sails for Tahiti where he marries a native woman only so that she can wait on him while he pursues his obsession. Based on the life of Paul Gauguin, Maugham's novel paints the portrait of an artist who flourished during the height of the decadent movement of the late nineteenth century and whose reckless style of living, if not indeed his unorthodox style of painting, owe more than a little to the decadent temper. Certainly in Maugham's novel we have a searing account of an unapologetic egoist who, in his disregard for everything but his art, causes anguish to all who come near him and ultimately does fatal harm to himself.

In *The Great Gatsby,* F. Scott Fitzgerald talks about the "careless people . . . who smashed up things and creatures and then retreated back into their money or their vast carelessness, or whatever it was that kept them together, and let other people clean up the mess they had made" (176). It is this "vast carelessness" that results in gratuitous suffering on the part of those who get caught in its wake. Martin Seymour-Smith maintains that it is Gatsby's "moral irresponsibility" that corrupts his genuine love (118). It is in "The Rich Boy," however, that Fitzgerald paints his most detailed portrait of a man who is the unself-conscious embodiment of "vast carelessness" and "moral irresponsibility." Anson Hunter has everything the common man despises (and covets): old money, privilege, social position, power, and most intolerable of all, an ingrained sense of superiority. That these things ultimately isolate Anson and turn him into a melancholy loner may seem like justice to some, but Fitzgerald refuses to gloat over what happens to Anson. Although this is not a compassionate portrait, it is an understanding one, for Anson cannot help being what he is. The women in his life suffer from his casual cruelty because they see in it something deliberate whereas we know that Anson does it unthinkingly, almost innocently.

The best illustration of Anson's thoughtless cruelty is the way he goes about terminating an affair between his Aunt Edna and her young lover, Cary Sloane. Because Anson fears the affair will ruin her marriage to his uncle Robert Hunter and thus damage the family name, he takes it upon himself to interfere. He puts such pressure on the lovers that his aunt has a nervous collapse and Cary Sloane commits suicide. Throughout the entire episode, Anson seems devoid of all feeling. Curiously enough, this very detachment has the effect of making his interference in their affair seem morally superior to the tawdriness of the affair itself, an affair which has all the trappings of cheap fiction.

While it is true that Anson sets about deliberately to put an end to this affair, he is totally unaware of the effect it is having on the parties involved. He honestly cannot feel what they feel. The only feeling he has is one of satisfaction at being able to handle a situation and be in control of other people's lives. He loves having the upper hand. This is why he takes a keen interest in the marriages of his friends, involving himself in the wedding arrangements and playing the role of counselor and confidant when things go wrong, listening patiently to their romantic and domestic problems and offering his advice. It is obvious, of course, that he does it for the sense of power it gives him, not because he really cares anything about the silly messes they get themselves involved in.

As with the other elements of decadence, decadent carelessness is a matter of extremes. If they are not busy interfering in others' lives, decadents are totally oblivious to the fact that others even exist. In this respect they behave like bad actors who cannot get the hang of the part they are trying to play, tearing up the scenery one moment, forgetting their lines the next. If they are writers, they operate on the comfortable assumption that writing is a one-way dialogue, with the author doing all the talking—or, if you will, the manipulating. When all those around them are simply their audience, they cease to see them as people. After that it is quite easy to cease to care about anything but their attention or their applause. People thus objectified become dehumanized.

"No man is an island," said Donne, and it may seem as if the decadents have forgotten. They haven't. They simply disagree. "A good friend," said Oscar Wilde, "is one who stabs you in the front." He also said that Judas writes your biography. Decadents believe that we live in a world where nobody owes anybody anything, where we are not our brother's keeper, and where every man *is* an island.

Chapter 6:

Strangers in Purgatory

The world is a stage, but the play is badly cast.

Oscar Wilde

Decadents feel that they are members of an estranged elite, trapped in limbo, "wandering," in Matthew Arnold's words, "between two worlds, one dead, the other powerless to be born" ("Stanzas," ll 85–86). To say that they are alienated does not do justice to their peculiar plight, for alienation is a word that is in danger of losing its meaning the more it is used to excuse antisocial behavior on the part of anyone from tomboys to terrorists. Even though it is still a useful word for describing the feeling of being out of step with society, it smacks too much of counterculture disaffection and self-pity to do justice to the decadents' feeling of being unwilling participants in a play that is not only badly cast but highly overrated.

If they want to, ordinary misfits can easily recant their antisocial attitudes and be welcomed back into society with open arms just as loners can choose to return to the fold the moment they decide they no longer want to be alone. But truly estranged persons are those who are on such a different wavelength from the world around them that there is really no fitting in, unless, of course, they choose to deceive themselves and everybody else. Such persons may truly want to belong—and would most probably be accepted—but they simply cannot bring themselves to conform without worrying that they have betrayed their instincts and compromised their integrity.

This principled, yet impassioned, sort of estrangement is a category limited enough to exclude the psychotic and the deranged as well as the criminally insane—anyone who is incapable of understanding the motives behind even an irrational decision. It also leaves out those who affect alienation merely as a way of setting themselves apart from the crowd, who enjoy being different only for the sake of being different. However, this description is also broad enough to go beyond the paranoia that alienation connotes to suggest the fierce pride of the estranged who feel that their estrangement has something in it of a vocation.

Decadent estrangement is based on feelings of profound regret, bewilderment, and disbelief. When decadents look about them, they see a travesty of rational or humanistic behavior. They see people pretending to care about others while grabbing all they can for themselves and defending extravagant indulgences as acts of rebellion against injustice. They see people taking up fashionable causes only as an excuse to feather their own nests. They see faddishness elevated to faith as illusions of immortality drive people to punish their bodies in the name of fitness. They see people more concerned about the duration than the quality of life, people who, in Oscar Wilde's phrase, "know the price of everything and the value of nothing."

Decadents find it ironic that what the world calls progress is really decay—and vice versa. They feel that they, whom the world labels decadent with the full force of the word's pejorative connotations, are the only ones who clearly see the decay and genuinely regret it. But since they feel in tune with the cycles of history, they do not believe that anything can or should be done to reverse the flow or, for that matter, even stem the tide.

This decadent ache for a mythical golden age becomes stronger as the present age becomes more disagreeable. "Feeling the desolateness of their own age, they develop a nostalgia for other places and other times," says Clyde Ryals. It is a peculiar sort of homesickness for a home they never knew, a home that exists in their imaginations rather than in their memories. In an age that seems increasingly hostile to tradition, he adds, decadents long "for a former age, for tradition and traditional value" (90). In *Against Nature,* Huysmans says that "when the period in which a man of talent is condemned to live is dull and stupid, the artist is haunted, perhaps unknown to himself, by a nostalgic yearning for another age" (181). Walter Pater called this nostalgia an "incurable thirst for the sense of escape, which no actual form of life satisfies" (*Appreciations,* 248). Implicit in this commentary is the speculation that much of decadent nostalgia is mere pose, a way of thumbing one's nose at the present by comparing it with one's own vision of Camelot.

In Evelyn Waugh's *Decline and Fall,* Paul Pennyfeather is in just such a wistful mood one summer morning as he stands among ancient chestnut trees in the park of a manor house and reflects on the past. "Surely, he thought, these great chestnuts in the morning sun stood for something enduring and serene in a world that had lost its reason and would so stand when the chaos and confusion were forgotten" (165).

In a world where the mad run free and think they are sane, where "The best lack all conviction, while the worst/Are full of passionate intensity," decadents do not wring their hands and weep with despair. Rather they withdraw discreetly to a position from which they can observe the fun, uncork the champagne, dip their toast points in caviar, and do their best to survive in style. Or, like Tibby in *Howards End,* they may retreat to the groves of academe and pursue a quiet life of undistinguished scholarship, far from the madding crowd.

Such a retreat is nowhere more fully realized than in Hermann Hesse's *Magister Ludi.* In this futuristic novel, its hero, Josef Knecht, succumbs to the allure of a remote academic sanctuary in which knowledge is pursued for its own sake free of the intrusions of mundane necessity. In his pursuit of the life of the mind, Knecht becomes the master of the bead game, an intellectual exercise that combines music and mathematics and which is purely esoteric. Knecht eventually discovers the dangers of living entirely for the spirit and leaves the sanctuary, but already it is too late. No longer capable of living in the everyday world, he dies an ironic death by drowning at the very moment he is attempting to immerse himself in the waters of life.

Hesse's *Demian* (1919) is also about the intense sort of alienation that illustrates decadent estrangement. In this novel, Emil Sinclair discovers that he is different from others—or at least he thinks he is—and this difference is aggravated by his friendship with the maguslike Max Demian, a totally self-possessed young man whose confidence encourages Sinclair to resist compromise. Demian boasts of wearing the mark of Cain as a symbol of the proud rebel who refuses to submit to the commonplace expectations of respectable society. Under the powerful spell of Demian and Demian's mother, Sinclair comes to accept Demian's god, the god Abraxas, half good, half evil, as his own. Alone with his visions, Sinclair experiences the isolation of decadent estrangement. Unfortunately, during the 1960s when *Demian* enjoyed a revival as a cult book of the counterculture, the mass identification with Sinclair and with Demian worked in direct opposition to Hesse's sublime individualism by turning estrangement into a communal affectation.

If an academic or religious retreat is out of the question, either for reasons of temperament or taste, decadents can, like Des Esseintes in *Against Nature,* turn their backs on society and pursue the unmolested life of an intellectual hermit. As a young man Des Esseintes tried his best to tolerate the young men of his own age and station, but he soon grew tired of those who had been brought up like himself. He thought of them as "docile, good-looking ninnies, congenital dunces" who had entered the world as the "pious, obedient creatures" their teachers had intended them to be. Likewise, he developed an immense distaste for the company of those who had been educated in state schools, for he found their debauchery "base and facile, entered into without discrimination or desire, indeed without any real stirring of the blood or stimulation of the nerves" (21).

Concluding at last that most people are nothing more than "fools and scoundrels," Des Esseintes abandons any hope of finding another person with

the same hopes and hates, another mind that prefers a life of "studious decrep-
itude," an intelligence "as sharp and wayward as his own" (22). All about him
are nothing but "mean mercenary minds" devoted to "swindling and money-
grubbing," narrow minds whose only other interest is in politics, "that igno-
ble distraction of mediocre intellects." But more than anything else, Des
Esseintes comes to hate with a passion the new breed of Philistines totally
lacking in tact or manner, those "appalling boors who find it necessary to talk
and laugh at the top of their voices in restaurants and cafés, who jostle you in
the street without a word of apology, and who, without expressing or even in-
dicating regret, drive the wheels of a baby-carriage into your legs" (39). If he
were to return a century later, he would see how little things have changed.

Des Esseintes has reached the point where he is "ripe for solitude, exhausted by life and expecting nothing more of it." Huysmans compares him
to a monk overcome by "an immense weariness, by a longing for peace and
quiet, by a desire to have no further contact with the heathen" (76). He feels
an affinity with those who escape to religious houses, driven there by an uncharitable society that resents their contempt for it and despises their attempt
to redeem it by pledging themselves to years of silence in atonement for the
"ever-increasing licentiousness of its silly, senseless conversations" (77).

"To be forced to be in harmony with others," says Lord Henry in *Dorian
Gray,* is the definition of discord. "One's own life—that is the important
thing." One's neighbors, he tells Dorian, are not one's concern. To become
concerned is to bully them with one's moral views, and that means conspiring
with one's age to follow its standards and foist them on others. "I consider that
for any man of culture to accept the standard of his age," says Lord Henry, "is a
form of the grossest immorality." Goodness, he says, is a matter of being "in
harmony with one's self" (227).

Richard Ellmann, in his biography of Wilde, calls such moral and intellectual exiles "aristocratic dilettantes" and points out that even when Wilde is
punishing them for being "detached and heartless," he is taking great delight
in them, for he undoubtedly sees their qualities in himself. Detached and
heartless they might very well be, but as far as they are concerned, they have
good reason. They have no peers, no equals. Let others call them decadent;
they accept no labels but their own, and they would be loath to join a cult or
become part of a deliberate movement. They are not joiners, and they care little for each other's company.

From what we know of Wilde's life and the life of his fictional double,
Lord Henry, Wilde felt that harmony with one's self could be achieved without the necessity of retreating from society. Both the author and his creation
are garrulous creatures who thrive in a social fishbowl, but we also know them
to be fiercely independent men whose wit, by managing to amuse and alienate
simultaneously, had the effect of insulating them from undue outside influence. This was also true of Truman Capote who craved crowds but felt in-

tensely alone in their midst, for frequently the people around him operated like mirrors in which he saw his own differences magnified.

Later, when Capote had grown disenchanted with the rich and was becoming increasingly neurotic about his reputation and fearful of his future, he was overcome by a nostalgia that, according to Gerald Clarke, "descended into sorrow." His writing, Clarke notes, had always been "tinged with nostalgia, a yearning for a serene and smiling past that he himself had not known, nor given to his fictional characters." But whereas others may experience a bitter-sweet pleasure from such feelings, in Capote nostalgia produced a pessimism "so profound that it darkened every waking moment." Capote admitted that the reason he did so many frivolous things was to try to escape the daily reminders of mutability and death. To those who knew him well during his last years, says Clarke, he seemed to be in "perpetual mourning, overwhelmed by a sense of loss that was no less keen because he could not say precisely what it was that had been taken from him" (402–403). This is the sense of unnameable loss that is at the heart of decadent estrangement.

In order to escape this sense of unnameable loss, the decadent personality seeks solace in solitude, but it is solitude, as Mann says in *Death in Venice*, that only aggravates the anguish. It is ironic, therefore, that Gustav Aschenbach's most acclaimed novel, *The Abject*, has as its theme the glorification of the splendid isolation of the artist. In this novel, says Mann, Aschenbach "rejects the rejected, casts out the outcast," renounces any "sympathy with the abyss" and quite flatly refutes the "flabby humanitarianism of the phrase: '*Tout comprendre c'est tout pardonner.*'" This is clearly the thinking of a mind that can tolerate no compromise, a mind that has lost touch with the moral equivalent of the principle of magnetic attraction. "What was here unfolding, or rather was already in full bloom," says Mann, "was the 'miracle of regained detachment'" (447).

If detachment is a blessing, it is at best a mixed one, and more likely to turn out to be a curse. Aschenbach, the writer who glorifies isolation, is eventually undone by the fact that his lifelong struggle to maintain that isolation must at last give way to its opposite: the desire to abandon the struggle and surrender to impulse. Under the spell of Venice and Tadzio, Aschenbach feels a yearning for that which is diametrically opposed to his art—and thus all the more alluring, a yearning for "the unorganized, the immeasurable, the eternal—in short, for nothingness." After all, says Mann in a statement laden with the bitter irony of intellectual rationalization, "he whose preoccupation is with excellence longs fervently to find rest in perfection; and is not nothingness a form of perfection?" (462).

Perfection is also what the diabolical hero of *Perfume* seeks—and virtually attains. But with it comes an unbearable estrangement which reaches its peak when he finds that the perfection he has achieved means nothing to the people it most affects. Here is a man who starts life as an outcast, a deformed bastard left to die in the gutters of Paris, but who manages to survive because of his genius for the art of perfumery. But he is mercilessly exploited, and by the time he finally breaks free and makes it on his own, he has arrived at the place where he trusts no one. Driven to depend totally on himself, he retreats from society and spends years alone in a cave until the solitude pushes him over the edge. After that, even when he pretends to fit in with a society that accepts him because of his talent, he sees through its pretenses and rages at its ignorance of the true nature of his genius.

When at last he eludes the executioner by releasing into the air the perfume that instigates the orgy among the spectators gathered to see him dismembered, he is deeply disappointed by the crowd's inability to appreciate the miracle of the perfume's manufacture. "No one knows how *well made* it is," he thinks to himself. Only he can recognize it for what it is, and that is because he is the one who has created it. Others surrender to its influence without even knowing that it is his perfume that is having such a hypnotic effect on them. The irony, for Grenouille, is that he alone is immune to its spell. "I am the only person," he laments, "for whom it is meaningless" (306).

Grenouille is suffering the agony of the artist who is acclaimed for the wrong reasons. No one understands that he murdered the young virgins because he "desired the scent, not the girl." Now, because the perfume he releases causes people to look up to him as they would look up to a savior, he deplores the fact that they believe they desire *him,* when what they really desire is a total mystery to them. It is ultimately this supreme irony that drives Grenouille to create and release the scent that carries people beyond adoration to murder and cannibalism.

In carrying the alienation of the estranged artist to such an extreme, Süskind goes farther than most modern writers in whose works one is less likely to encounter such a virulent strain of this particular element of decadence. While still holding society in contempt, modern decadents are more likely to enjoy observing its folly, to approach it as something they love to hate. It is this sort of love-hate attitude that characterizes most of the modern writers who take a jaundiced view of the world around them. They become neither recluses nor martyrs. Rather they prefer the pose that best sums up the decadent attitude: sardonic aloofness.

Perhaps the best exemplar of this attitude is Tom Wolfe, a writer who is able to become what can only be described as an "invisible presence" in the midst of things, seeing but unseen, included but not involved. In so doing, he operates somewhat like the spy who smiles amiably at an embassy cocktail party while wearing a microphone in his lapel and secretly plotting the overthrow of the host government. This was Tom Wolfe's stance when, in a London restaurant in 1969, he met Germaine Greer, a woman who was to become one of those most strident voices in contemporary literary criticism, particularly feminist criticism. At the time, Ms. Greer was co-editor of *Suck,* a newspaper along the lines of its American counterpart *Screw.* As Wolfe describes it, "*Suck* was full of pictures of gaping things, moist lips, stiffened giblets, glistening nodules, dirty stories, dirty poems, essays on sexual freedom, and a gossip column detailing the sexual habits of people whose names I assumed were fictitious" (*Purple,* 287).

Sleazy as the magazine was, Wolfe was even more intrigued by Ms. Greer's outlandish appearance and behavior. He describes her as a "thin, hard-looking woman with a tremendous curly electric hairdo and the most outrageous Naugahyde mouth I had ever seen on a woman." As he sat there in the restaurant with Ms. Greer and her co-editor Jim Haynes, Ms. Greer "got bored and set fire to her hair with a match." The frantic attempt on the part of two waiters to beat out the flames with napkins made a noise, Wolfe says, "like pigeons taking off in the park." Ms. Greer just sat there "with a sublime smile on her face" while Jim Haynes continued to discourse on the aims of *Suck* which were liberation of the spirit of man through sexual liberation (288).

Tom Wolfe could not believe his ears—or his eyes. He kept watching Jim Haynes's face

for the beginning of a campy grin, a smirk, a wink, a roll of the eyeballs—something to indicate that he was just having his little joke. But it soon became clear that he was one of those people who exist on a plane quite . . . Beyond Irony. Whatever it had been for him once, sex had now become a religion, and he had developed a theology in which the orgasm had become a form of spiritual ecstasy (288).

It is the distance between the many who exist on a plane "Beyond Irony" and the few who do not that is the measure of decadent estrangement in modern times. Ironic detachment has always been the hallmark of decadent estrangement, but in Wolfe's case, instead of being on the outside looking in, he is on the inside looking out. It is this altered angle of perception, along with his detachment, that gives Tom Wolfe's social satires their decadent flavor.

The paradox of being a part of what one perceives and yet not having any real effect on what is happening is what gives a decadent dimension to new journalism, an approach to reporting that Tom Wolfe is credited with having invented. Certainly he knows better than anyone how to convey the feeling, so important to new journalism, of a dreamlike inability to alter the events one is witnessing, even participating in. Truman Capote, who added to the stature of the new journalism approach by using it with such chilling effect in *In Cold Blood,* got interested in journalism precisely because this new trend allowed him to stand up close to reality and yet remain, as it were, invisible. "I like the feeling that something is happening beyond and about me and I can do nothing about it," he said shortly before he came upon the news item that led to investigation of the Clutter family murders. "I like having the truth be the truth so I can't change it" (Clarke, 317). The trouble is that those about whom the unchangeable truth is told would often give anything—or do anything—to change, if not indeed cancel, that truth.

Much as they may cherish their detachment, decadents have been known to crave fame, even notoriety. Oscar Wilde's American tour in the early 1880s was a demonstration of his fondness for publicity; and whenever public attention did not automatically come his way, he courted it shamelessly. Later he got a good deal of notoriety by deliberately putting himself in a position to be humiliated. In many ways, Truman Capote followed in Wilde's footsteps. In his biography of Capote, Gerald Clarke gives us an engaging and sometimes infuriating portrait of a modern decadent who, like Oscar Wilde, courted shamelessly the very audience from whom he felt estranged and whom he eventually managed to alienate. In his review of Clarke's biography, John Skow sums up Capote as a person who "lived an outrageous life, mostly against society's grain, and invented gaudy lies to pad out the occasional dull spots" (*Time,* 60). Like so many decadents, Capote was his own invention and his own greatest advertiser. Estranged from the ordinary world by his odd looks, his high voice, his bizarre sexual tastes, and his genius, he, like Oscar Wilde in real life and Jean-Baptiste Grenouille in fiction, provoked his public into ostracizing him and then blamed them for mistreating him. He brought ignominy upon himself and then berated the public for its disapproval.

When he was a child, Capote's mother used to lock him in a hotel room while she went galavanting for long periods of time, and he once said of this experience: "She locked me in and I still can't get out" (Clarke, 400). Like Capote, decadents feel locked in, trapped, unable to escape. Combine this claustrophobic loneliness with an exaggerated sense of self-importance (Capote thought of his writing as "true art" as opposed to "good writing") and a jaundiced view of the world, and you have a darker side of decadent estrangement, a curious desolation that all attempts to remedy only make more painful.

What Walter Pater said more than a century ago about Marius in *Marius, the Epicurean* could easily be said about decadent writers of modern times. Like Marius, they are seeking rescue from "the vulgarity and heaviness of a generation of no general fineness of temper [but] with a material well-being abundant enough" (141). And like Marius they are convinced that "interaction with the world outside is not possible." One hears Capote's voice in Marius's lament that there is no getting "beyond the walls of the closely shut cell of one's own personality" (141). The ideas that we form of the outer world, and of kindred minds, are, to Marius, only a daydream, and the thought of any world beyond that daydream is itself an even idler daydream.

It is just such an "idle daydream" that Daphne du Maurier dares to imagine in *The House on the Strand,* a novel that speaks to modern disenchantment with life gone stale. Daphne du Maurier, known mostly for her Gothic romances, especially the classic *Rebecca,* surprised her readers in 1969, in much the same way Graham Greene had surprised his just a year before, by writing a book that seemed out of character, a book that was a marked departure from what either had done before. In Greene's case it was *Travels with My Aunt,* a black comedy with an outlandish plot, a wry mockery of a new generation of writers who thought they had a monopoly on the bizarre. In du Maurier's case it was *The House on the Strand,* a novel based on experimentation with drugs on the part of a weak but sympathetic main character.

In both novels, one still finds the distinctive stylistic flourishes and familiar landscapes: Greene's sardonic humor and du Maurier's Cornish chauvinism. What is different in both cases is primarily a matter of tone. Both books seem unusually indulgent and innovative, as if the sixties had presented their authors with a challenge, and they were out to prove that they were a better match for it than anyone might imagine. Interestingly enough, there are decadent overtones in both books, but it is the du Maurier novel that is a veritable parable of estrangement.

Decadence has always had more than just a passing flirtation with things Gothic, and elements of decadence can be found in many of du Maurier's works, especially some of her shorter fiction such as "Don't Look Back" and in a novel like *My Cousin Rachel.* But *The House on the Strand,* with its selfishness and masochism, its estrangement and perversity, its irresponsibility and regret, remains du Maurier's most conspicuously decadent novel, a verdict that Miss du Maurier, granddaughter of George du Maurier, author of *Trilby* and creator of that arch-manipulator, Svengali, might just be disposed to agree with.

In *The House on the Strand,* its hero, Dick Kilmarth, is poking about in the cellar of the Kilmarth ancestral home in Cornwall when he comes across a vial containing a strange substance. This substance, which resembles LSD, has the effect of transporting him back to the fourteenth century, just before the onset of the Black Plague, where he becomes voyeuristically involved in the lives of the people who inhabited this stretch of the Cornish coast at that time, particularly those ancestors of his who inhabited Kilmarth.

At first Dick is so shaken by the nauseating aftereffects of the drug that he swears never to try it again. However, his initial experience is so overwhelming that he knows he must repeat it no matter how horrible the aftereffects might be. And the more he finds modern life unsatisfying, the more he is tempted to return to a time when people and events seemed bigger than life. Dick is married to an American named Vita who has two sons from a previous marriage. Vita is one of du Maurier's ugly American women, brassy and unfeeling, and her sons are indolent and spoiled. But beyond that there is the pervasive dullness of modern life with its busywork and doubtful pleasures, its trivializing of values, its reducing of life to a sequence of missed planes and lost luggage, of cramped cars and crowded roads, of tiresome small talk and tedious television.

In contrast, the life of the fourteenth century is given the sweep and pageantry of an Elizabethan drama. Daphne du Maurier, with her flair for historical fiction and her devotion to Cornwall, is able to bring that distant drama to life and give it such immediacy that Dick's preference for those times becomes quite understandable. Ultimately, Dick is psychologically unable to remain in the twentieth century even though he knows that if he returns, he will be returning to an England just about to be ravaged by the Black Death. Of course, during his rational periods he knows full well that it is all hallucination and that he is killing himself, but, like Gustav Aschenbach, he has long since crossed over the line to self-destruction. Whatever the explanation, whatever the consequences, he prefers to "burn with a gemlike flame" in the glorious past, even if it is a dream, rather than to die of boredom in what is called reality. Thus, as the novel ends and he puts Vita and the children on the plane to America (to him—as to du Maurier—a fate worse than death!) and promises to follow soon, it is clear that he cannot wait to get back to Kilmarth, back to the substance in the bottle down there in the basement, back to Roger and Isolde and the life of medieval Cornwall.

Dick's disillusionment with modern life, his disappointment over what has been lost with the passing of history, his wish to escape the life he is now living, to get as far away from it as possible, especially in terms of time, is a vivid illustration of decadent estrangement. At one point he reminds himself that he is powerless to interfere with the events of the time-trips he takes and that his responsibility is to the present and to the people who depend on him. But the reminder only depresses him. He despises obligations, loathes responsibilities. Like Truman Capote, he wants to be presented with circumstances he cannot possibly alter.

Si Morley, the narrator of Jack Finney's *Time and Again,* is very similar to Dick Kilmarth in his desire to return to the past as mere observer, but eventually his reason changes and he ends up going back with every intention of altering the course of history. Si Morley, an illustrator living in the 1980s, gets involved in a government scheme to return selected persons to earlier time periods for the purpose of affecting history. Morley travels back in time to the New York of the 1880s, but once he arrives there he is reluctant to leave. He is also reluctant to do the government's bidding and try to change things until, on a return visit to the present, a modern event occurs that he thinks he might, after all, like to prevent if he can just get back in time. He does, but he also becomes so obsessed with what he takes to be the simpler world of the 1880s— before world wars, before mass pollution, before rampant crime—that he ends up staying. "This, too, was an imperfect world," he says, "but—I drew a deep breath, sharply chill in my lungs—the air was still clean. The rivers flowed fresh, as they had since time began. And the first of the terrible corrupting wars still lay decades ahead" (398).

When C.E.M. Joad accuses the decadents of misreading their place in the universe, it is the wildly extreme view of one's place in the universe that he is referring to, an egocentric view that only the humility and compassion of a saint could render palatable to the multitudes. "I exaggerate everything," says Dostoyevsky's underground man; "that's where I go wrong" (203). He may pretend at times to have genuine concern for the lot of his fellow man, but one would be hard pressed to find a spark of brotherly love in his relentless spitefulness. Even his dreams of sacrificing himself for "the good and the beautiful" sound more like grandiose delusions calculated to shame his enemies and bring glory upon himself than like genuine hope for the salvation of mankind. "Everyone would kiss me and weep," he says as he fantasizes himself bringing the good and the beautiful to the people, and then adds in parenthesis: "(what idiots they would be if they didn't)" (164).

Like Des Esseintes in *Against Nature,* the underground man is disgusted with the mechanical mentality that would subordinate man to a machine. He has nothing but contempt for the technological optimism of the nineteenth century and the concept that men are ciphers in neat equations. "The whole work of man," he thinks, "really seems to consist in nothing but proving to himself every minute that he is a man and not a piano-key" (146). He wants to thumb his nose for the sake of thumbing it, for that is what freedom is all about; and he finds the idea rather charming that two and two might, after all, equal five.

Dostoyevsky himself saw the underground man as Russia's salvation, if only Russia would welcome such an independent spirit instead of casting him out. It would seem, however, that his hero is not likely to trust any overtures of friendship from a society that pretends to be reasonable but which, as far as he is concerned, acts irrationally. This is also Des Esseintes's complaint: that society accuses him of its own worst faults, calling him irrational when, in fact, it is society that is not only utterly irrational but viciously hypocritical.

Decadent estrangement stems from a tragic view of life that experience only heightens until one is forced to stand apart in "terrible, splendid isolation" (Beckson, xxxix) and "to become the spectator of one's own life" in an attempt "to escape the suffering of life" (*Dorian,* 263). Truman Capote's experiences with the two killers whose story he tells in *In Cold Blood* served to heighten his own tragic view of life, a view he says he had always held and which, in his words, accounts "for the side of me that appears extremely frivolous; that part of me [that] is always standing in a darkened hallway, mocking tragedy and death. That's why I love champagne and stay at the Ritz" (*Conversations,* 124).

Isak Dinesen's life is a case study in estrangement. As a young woman she longed to break the ties that confined her to the stifling restrictions of bourgeois Denmark. Her father, who had traveled to America and lived among the Indians in Wisconsin, had given her a model to follow, and when he committed suicide, she saw it as a means of escape. When the chance came to marry and go to Africa, she grabbed it even though it meant marrying a man she did not love and who infected her with a venereal disease that ruined her health. Late in life she said it had been worth it, for, among other things, it had enabled her to escape to Africa.

However, Africa proved to be, in its own way, another sort of confinement, for regardless of the liberation she managed to experience and to distill into the exquisite memoir *Out of Africa,* her letters home during that seventeen-year ordeal reveal the almost unbearable pressures she was enduring. The farm continued to lose money as either the coffee crop or the coffee market failed. Meanwhile, her marriage broke up, her health deteriorated, and the man she loved deeply, Denys Finch-Hatton, died in a plane crash. As she herself said, in so many words, Africa was an "answered prayer" in the most ironic meaning of the phrase.

Even during this period, Dinesen had to make frequent trips back to Denmark for treatment of her disease, and while she was there, she was confined most of the time to her room at Rungstedlund, the room in which she had been born and in which she would eventually die. She lived the life of a virtual prisoner, since her disease was a closely kept secret, and later, when she returned home for good once she could no longer stay on in Africa, she virtually locked herself in her room for two years while she wrote *Seven Gothic Tales,* gambling on the remote chance that anyone in the midst of a world-wide depression would be interested in "decadent" fairy tales. When the book actually did become a success in America and England, she became an outcast in Denmark for her pretensions, and when *Seven Gothic Tales* appeared in a Danish edition, she suffered the scorn of critics who tolerated only novels of grim social realism and who looked upon her writing as wicked and perverse.

Time has done much to heal the schism between Dinesen and her Danish compatriots, although much of it has to do with her international reputation, something the Danes can hardly afford to ignore. But there remains a lurking suspicion among her countrymen that she is pulling the wool over somebody's eyes. What they are not quite sure of is whether this wool is being pulled over the eyes of her uncritical foreign readers who refuse to see what a silly snob she was or over the eyes of the Danes who are loath to acknowledge the fact that it is against them that she has always been in revolt. Her biographer, Judith Thurman, feels that Dinesen has much in common with *fin-de-siècle* decadents like Huysmans and Villiers de l'Isle-Adam, who were estranged from their society, and that her affinity with them "has less to do with the way her characters cross-dress, or abuse the pleasures of the flesh, than with their and her own sense of being trapped and alienated by civilized (bourgeois) life" (268).

In *The Social History of Art,* Arnold Hauser suggests a context in which decadent estrangement can be better understood. To him, decadence "is the consciousness of standing at the end of a vital process and in the presence of the dissolution of a civilization." He sees decadence as an intensification of "Byronic weariness" and "the romantic passion for death," and argues that "the same abyss attracts both the romantic and the decadent" and that it is "the same delight in destruction, self-destruction, that intoxicates them. But for the decadent," he adds, "everything is an abyss" (888). For the Christian this abyss was sin, for the knight, dishonesty, and for the bourgeois, illegality, he says, but for the decadent, it is "everything for which he lacks concepts, words, and formulae" (889). This explains why decadents love form and ritual and why they feel increasingly alienated as society continues to move toward social anarchy.

"We are born into a world where alienation awaits us," says R.D. Laing in *The Politics of Experience* (xv). Although he is not referring specifically to decadents, what he says could easily be the first item of the decadent credo. In the decadent consciousness, this alienation is a burden thrust upon one, a burden made all the worse by the fact that it is a burden one does not particularly care to shoulder. Thus, the torment created by the tension between the desire for complete indifference and the nagging anxiety that cannot be dismissed, between not caring at all and caring too much—that feeling of standing in the darkened hallway mocking tragedy and death, of seeing the eternal footman snicker—this torment results in the special kind of agonized estrangement which is peculiar to the decadent sensibility. For the decadent is simultaneously the superman of Shaw and Nietzsche and the superfluous man of Goncharov, Dostoyevsky, and Kafka, the man who praises himself too highly one moment and punishes himself too severely the next.

Chapter 7:

In Pursuit of Pain

Cruel and unusual . . . words to live by.

Paul Rudnick, *Social Disease*

Suffering is certainly not new to literature. Without it there would be no *Odyssey*, no *Oedipus Rex*, no *Divine Comedy*, no *Hamlet*. But the pleasure that can be derived from suffering—from causing it, of course, but especially from experiencing it oneself—is a theme that finds its fullest expression in the novel. Right from the beginning the novel, because of its intimacy and length, had the leisure to strip away layers of feeling and expose every sensitive nerve. Samuel Richardson, whose *Pamela* is generally considered to be the first fully realized novel, literally invented the novel of sentiment in which feeling is foremost and suffering paramount.

In the eighteenth century suffering was a sign of virtue; the more you suffered, the better person you were. And no one suffers like Clarissa Harlowe, the heroine of Richardson's second novel. Clarissa's persecution by her seducer, Robert Lovelace, drags on through a dozen volumes and ends with Clarissa writing her last frantic epistles using her own coffin as an escritoire. The plight of the suffering heroine continued through the Gothic romances of popular writers like Anne Radcliffe (*The Mysteries of Udolpho*), but it found its most artistic expression in such nineteenth-century classics as Charlotte Brontë's *Jane Eyre,* Flaubert's *Madame Bovary,* and Tolstoy's *Anna Karenina,* as well as in a host of lesser works such as Kate Chopin's *The Awakening.*

Such prolonged and excessive suffering may have a decadent flavor to it; however, it is really too much of a romantic literary convention to be so narrowly defined. Its importance to decadence lies, rather, in the fact that this literary emphasis on the pleasure of pain actually owes as much to the Marquis de Sade as it does to Samuel Richardson—and some, like Mario Praz, say that it owes even more. It was, after all, de Sade, that brilliant but depraved scholar of the perverse, who made us see that pain can be pleasureful, and after him the motif of suffering took on new and darker dimensions in western literature. But even here, the emphasis was on giving pain, not receiving it, and the sufferers could point accusing fingers at their torturers for finding pleasure in making their victims suffer.

Then, in the mid-nineteenth century, a neurotic Austrian novelist by the name of Leopold Sacher-Masoch began writing novels in which the characters actually enjoy their suffering, even go out of their way to provoke it. Certainly the distraught heroines of much of Victorian fiction seem to bring a great deal of their suffering on themselves and to go out of their way to prolong it. There is little in it, however, of the withering self-abasement that characterizes the decadent extremes to which suffering can be carried when the sufferer is his own victim and believes that he deserves his punishment.

Separately, sadism and masochism produce stereotypes such as the tyrannical Victorian father and his long-suffering daughter (Elizabeth Barrett Browning and her father in Wimpole Street; Dr. Sloper and his daughter in *Washington Square*). Combined into sadomasochism, these two strains produce the abused and abusive sadomasochistic hero of Dostoyevsky's *Notes from Underground* and similar characters since. The observations of both de Sade and Sacher-Masoch have long since entered the mainstream of modern thought, of course, and the behavior they described has become a familiar feature of modern literature. Their relationship to decadence, however, has been misunderstood. It is wrong to think that decadence is a taste for whips and chains or bondage and slavery. If this were so, then a case could be made for applying the label of decadent to everything from the boys' schools of Dickens's day, to Marine boot camp, to the "no pain, no gain" philosophy of the health enthusiast. What de Sade and Sacher-Masoch contributed to decadence is an attitude toward pain that is in some ways similar to the attitude of certain religions towards mortification of the flesh. The difference is that for the devout, suffering is a means of spiritual awakening, whereas for the decadent, suffering is a means of purging some ineradicable guilt, of paying the penalty for having a low opinion of the world and of oneself, of punishing oneself as a way of punishing the world. For masochism is as much an act of rebellion as it is an act of faith. Self-abasement is, after all, the inverse of egoism.

Decadent suffering, as we have seen, is more likely to be emotional than physical, a matter of nerves and feelings and what used to be called "spleen": in a word, neurotic. Such suffering is usually motivated by self-loathing, but since self-loathing is the counter image of self-love, it is not always easy to tell which emotion is in control or if the two are not, in fact, working in tandem. As the narrator of Dostoyevsky's *Notes from Underground* says: "I, for instance, have a great deal of *amour propre*. I am as suspicious and prone to take offense as a hunchback, or a dwarf. But, upon my word, I sometimes have had moments when, if I had happened to be slapped in the face, I should, perhaps, have been positively glad of it" (129). After all, he says, "man is sometimes extraordinarily, passionately in love with suffering, and that's a fact, for suffering is the sole origin of consciousness" (148).

In order, then, to find the most immediate source of decadent suffering, we must look but to Dostoyevsky, and in particular to the manic-depressive hero of *Notes from Underground*. André Gide and Thomas Mann both paid tribute to this novel for its delineation of a deeper strain of personal anguish, and Sigmund Freud, in *Dostoyevsky and Parricide,* analyzed it as the product of the author's own urge to punish himself as well as his need to be punished based upon an intense sense of unfathomable guilt. In his introduction to this novel, Charles Neider says that the work's greatness resides in the tension which stems from the hero's "sense of guilt and his efforts to expiate for [his] unknown crime" (18). This same tension and this same sense of guilt for an unknown crime reappear much later in Kafka's *The Trial,* the twentieth century's definitive expression of the decadent mania for self-punishment.

Neider notes that Dostoyevsky's hero, "pendulating between sadism and masochism, outdragoning the world one moment and outflunkying it another," is in the grips of impulses "which are often 'unreasonable' to the extent of being suicidal" (19). It is important to keep in mind that it is the extreme nature of this paranoia that makes it decadent. Ordinary guilt and its accompanying need for punishment are the correctives that conscience applies to what would otherwise be morally objectionable behavior. When guilt and punishment are stretched beyond ordinary endurance, however, the will is either paralyzed or inimical. The person harboring the guilt may feel powerless to act in any positive way to expiate the guilt, or he may feel caught between the desire to resist and the desire to cooperate. Part of him wants to get back at his mostly imaginary persecutors while another part wants to assist them in their persecution of him by giving them cause, either by committing the crime he is being accused of or by assuming that he already has given sufficient offense to warrant the punishment that is being meted out.

Dostoyevsky's underground man goes out of his way to make a nuisance of himself, deliberately inviting abuse and then resenting it, while on another level he is welcoming it and believing that he fully deserves it. He goads others into insulting him or ignoring him or pulling things on him and then spends his time whining about the way he is being treated and plotting revenge against those who treat him that way. This revenge usually takes the form of making himself even more obnoxious to them the next time he runs into them. He lets insults fester for years on end, frequently going out of his way to incur them by taking walks on streets where he knows he will be ignored and brushed aside. One particularly painful stroll he describes as "a series of innumerable miseries, humiliations and resentments; but no doubt that was just what I wanted," he adds. He calls the experience "a regular martyrdom; a continual, intolerable humiliation," but he feels drawn there at every possible opportunity. "Why I inflicted this torture upon myself," he cries, "I don't know" (160).

The underground world of this tormented man is as much a symbol of cloistered retreat as the ivory tower of Josef Knecht's Castalia in Hermann Hesse's *Magister Ludi*. Dostoyevsky's hero, like Hesse's, is cut off from the larger world, but whereas Knecht's world is remote and spacious, the world of the underground man is cramped and cloying. He rarely goes out, and the only people he sees, in addition to those irritating pedestrians who take no notice of him, are the few acquaintances on whom he forces himself, the servant he lets abuse him, and Lisa, the prostitute whose moral superiority brings out the worst in him. For while part of him is toadying to those he despises, another part is reminding him of how much better he is than the age in which he lives, regardless of how he is perceived. "I was a mere fly in the eyes of all this world," he says, "a nasty, disgusting fly—more intelligent, more highly developed, more refined in feeling than any of them—but a fly that was continually making way for everyone, insulted and injured by everyone" (160).

The rejection by society that the underground man encourages is a reminder to him of his superiority, something he feels he naturally possesses but which, at the same time, he does not really deserve. His behavior suggests that he secretly envies the life he scorns. However, unlike the saint who can reject worldly temptation for the promise of heavenly rewards, the decadent has no refuge awaiting him, no reward to anticipate for resisting temptation or for withstanding rebuke. Thus, his suffering is all the more painful and all the more exquisite.

This is Des Esseintes's problem. Throughout *Against Nature* he torments himself by basing his behavior on a rejection of all he despises in society. Whereas a pious man would simply turn his back on the world and meditate on spiritual matters, Des Esseintes is totally preoccupied with the world he loathes but cannot turn away from. He mocks it, he mimics it, he carries its inanities to extremes. What he cannot do is ignore it, and thus he is miserable. Toward the end of the book, his mental and physical health have both deteriorated to the point where he can no longer take comfort in the pessimism of Schopenhauer or in the maxim of Pascal to the effect that "the soul sees nothing that does not distress it on reflection" (219).

Des Esseintes has reached the nadir of distress and realizes at last that "the arguments of pessimism were powerless to comfort him, that only the impossible belief in a future life could bring him peace of mind" (219). Huysmans' friend and fellow author Barbey d'Aurevilly told him that after writing this novel Huysmans would have to choose between "the muzzle of a pistol and the foot of the cross" (Huysmans,12). Des Esseintes, at the end of the book, chooses the cross and throws himself on God's mercy, begging God to erase his doubts and restore his faith. His disciple, Dorian Gray, after torturing himself with repeated visits to the attic where he has hidden the hateful portrait that reveals the extent of his monstrous depravity, chooses suicide when he stabs his portrait and, in so doing, kills himself.

Since the pursuit of pleasure is sometimes indistinguishable from the pursuit of pain, it is not surprising that what starts out as one can end up as the other. When Gustav Aschenbach in *Death in Venice* sets off on his journey to Italy, his avowed intent is to take a holiday from the rigors of authorship. He is ostensibly in search of a pleasureful interlude, a happy distraction from the discipline of work. What he encounters in Venice is the pain of degradation, and the more he gives in to it, the more he accepts his shame and enjoys his humiliation. He accepts the cholera epidemic and the threat of death with morbid delight and lets the perverse thrill of his infatuation with the Polish boy, Tadzio, gladden his frenzied soul. He courts disaster at every turn as he tracks the boy through the dank and narrow alleyways of Venice, daring to be found out, to be challenged, to be shamed. His hair dyed black, his face powdered, his cheeks rouged, Aschenbach turns himself into a grotesque parody of the idea of beauty to which he has at last surrendered, the ideal which causes him to reject a lifetime of intellectual pursuit and literary achievements for the ecstasy of degradation.

There comes a moment in Aschenbach's anguished infatuation when he comes perilously close to touching Tadzio, to speaking to him, but he manages to pull back just in time even though taking this perilous step might have burst the bubble of his fantasy and had the effect of waking him from a dream before the dream descended into nightmare. In short, a touch or a word could have led to his recovery, but Mann speculates that perhaps Aschenbach did not really want to be cured, that perhaps he cherished his illusion more than his sanity. Who understands the riddle of the artist's nature, "that mingling of discipline and license in which it stands so deeply rooted?" asks Mann. The danger is to be beyond wanting sobriety, he says, "for not to be able to want sobriety is licentious folly" (475). Yet by this time Aschenbach is no longer capable of knowing his own mind or controlling his own impulses. He is beyond caring about what is happening to him. He has become too arrogant to admit emotion, let alone admit the fear of it, and therefore he lets emotion destroy him. When he is on the point of leaving Venice and a baggage mix-up gives him a chance to change his mind, he seizes the opportunity with alacrity and returns to his hotel, eagerly surrendering to his tragic fate.

Anguished preoccupation with oneself is to modern literature what the suffering heroine was to Victorian, and it is as likely to be found in the creators of decadent characters as in the characters they create. From Marcel Proust's neurotic seclusion in a cork-lined bedroom in Paris to Truman Capote's pathetic conversations with himself, we have become accustomed to the presence of tortured souls who carry on a debilitating love-hate relationship with the world—and with themselves—and who often are destroyed in the process.

Franz Kafka, the twentieth century's leading literary authority on the paranoid personality, is also its leading purveyor of psychological masochism. Kafka knew the paralysis of fear and self-loathing firsthand, and his early death, while directly attributable to tuberculosis, was hastened by the despair brought on by this paralysis, a despair he projected so brilliantly in the neurotic nightmares of his characters' paranoid imaginations. In his biography of Kafka, *The Nightmare of Reason,* Ernst Pawel speaks of Kafka's "volcanic self-hatred" and says that Kafka hated himself "not for being a Jew, but for not being enough of one" (400–401).

Pawel tells us that even as a young man Kafka sincerely believed himself to be "incompetent, lazy, forgetful, clumsy"—the list goes on—"as self-disdain yielded to self-hatred" (53). This merciless self-criticism continued throughout his life, but Pawel notes that "there is a curious undertone of perverse complacency, almost of pride to the strident insistence with which he flaunts his faults." In Pawel's opinion, "Kafka's self-deprecation served a clearly defensive purpose: it removed him from the contest, put him out of danger's reach, and enabled him to 'disappear' at the crucial moment of confrontation" (53). This is the escape route the decadent likes to keep open. He may cavil at society, but he is quick to take cover behind his own advertised weaknesses when action is called for—or, for that matter, his bluff is called.

Part of the decadent penchant for self-abasement also has something to do with envying those with better looks and fitter physiques or those with better manners and sharper wits. Dostoyevsky's underground man detests Zvercov, the officer whose farewell dinner he ruins, for all these reasons. Zvercov's reputation for tact and social polish particularly infuriates him, but he also hates the "abrupt self-confident tone of his voice, [and] his admiration of his own witticisms, which," he says, "were often frightfully stupid." But most of all, he says, he hates Zvercov's "handsome but stupid face," and then hastens to add that it is a face "for which I would have gladly exchanged my intelligent one" (167).

Kafka's intense interest in exercise and matters of health is apt to puzzle those who see him as a tubercular neurotic, pale and distraught, scribbling away at his psychological horror stories far from sunlight and fresh air and decent food. The truth is that he exercised daily, participated in outdoor sports, even forced himself to go on long marches, and he was well known for running around in the dead of winter without coat or gloves. He even became a vegetarian. Pawel sees all of this as a "grim resolve to punish the body for what it was or, more precisely, for not being what some part of him felt it ought to be: a healthy animal in a happy herd" (205–206). Meanwhile, he was still castigating himself, as in this letter to Felice Bauer, a woman with whom he was romantically involved: "I am a nothing, an absolute nothing. . . . I have never met anyone more hopelessly inadequate than I" (293–294). Pawel interprets his writing as a form of self-mutilation, as one more way to torture himself in the ongoing battle of "Kafka-versus-Kafka." It is almost as if writing for him was like placing himself under the harrow of the diabolical machine in "The Penal Colony."

Nowhere is the vanity of self-loathing more vividly presented than in the transformation of Gregor Samsa into a giant cockroach in Kafka"s "The Metamorphosis." Gregor is a little slow to catch on to just how repulsive he looks, but as he begins to perceive this in the reactions of others, it only confirms the feelings of self-loathing that brought on this condition, and he comes to despise himself even more than others do. Of course, occasionally he gets impulses to jump out at people and frighten them, impulses that are much like the contrariness of the narrator of *Notes from Underground;* but for the most part Gregor is so protective of the feelings of others that he hides himself from them so that they will not be upset by his disgusting appearance.

If this were a religious experience, Gregor would eventually become spiritually restored. But it is a relentlessly secular experience, and Gregor is not saved. Ironically enough, however, his family is rejuvenated once he is gone because, having learned that they do not need him to lean on, they discover a new and vigorous independence. Although they are the beneficiaries of what has happened to him, his suffering means nothing to them, and his ignominious death only points up his worthlessness and the fact that his life had been superfluous. He would have been better off never to have lived at all, a Calvinist paradox with more than a hint of decadent ambiguity.

Closer in spirit to the decadent addiction to suffering are the central characters in Kafka's *The Trial* and *The Castle.* The main character in *The Castle,* a man known only as K., suffers the torment of eternal delays in his attempt to visit a seemingly inaccessible castle and eventually despairs of ever being granted the permission he seeks. K.'s torment is similar to that of Des Esseintes, whose desire to be admitted into the realm of the faithful is as doomed as K.'s desire to be admitted into the inner sanctum of the castle. It is in *The Trial,* however, that the willing acceptance of pain is most evident. In this novel, a man named Joseph K. is arrested one day for an unspecified crime and spends the rest of the book tirelessly battling the legal bureaucracy in an attempt to discover the nature of his crime. While the agonies of a pointless search become the substance of his life, the growing conviction that he is guilty of some crime or other takes possession of him, and eventually he welcomes his own execution.

Renunciation is another manifestation of decadent masochism. The pleasure of renunciation comes from renouncing pleasure, from backing off and showing the world that one is superior to pleasure.

To the decadents, renunciation is as perverse as licentiousness. Lord Henry tells Dorian Gray that when we renounce, "we degenerate into hideous puppets, haunted by the memory of the passions of which we were too much afraid, and the exquisite temptations that we had not the courage to yield to" (165). When Lord Henry sends Dorian a copy of *Against Nature,* Dorian is quite taken by the description of its hero, the young Parisian who loves "for their mere artificiality those renunciations that men have unwisely called virtue, as much as those natural rebellions that wise men still call sin" (280).

Dorian, however, misses Des Esseintes's point. He does not fully understand the peculiar psychology of renunciation, which he thinks of as deprivation at too great a price. Wilde tells us that Dorian is "haunted by a feeling of loss" at how much sensual pleasure has been surrendered throughout history and to such little purpose, and he reflects sadly on the bitter irony of all those "mad wilful rejections" and those "monstrous forms of self-torture and self-denial" that have been committed solely out of fear and that have only resulted in a degradation far more terrible than any degradation they might have fooled themselves into thinking they had escaped (286). To see renunciation as more depraved than profligacy is mere sophistry; to *prefer* renunciation precisely because it *is* more depraved is decadence. Toward the end of *Dorian Gray* there is a hint that Dorian is about ready to abandon his sinful life, but his time runs out before he gets around to doing it. Even if he had renounced worldly pleasure, however, it would have been more out of boredom and fatigue than out of a desire to feel morally superior by turning his back at the moment when temptation was most persistent.

This idea of renunciation as a form of masochism raises questions about Henry James and the recurrence of this theme in so many of his novels and short stories. Certainly there is an unmistakable sense of joy in the eagerness with which so many of his characters choose a life of passive detachment over one of active involvement. In "The Beast in the Jungle," John Marcher ultimately renounces life in favor of an illusion, in his case the illusion that life has destined him for greatness and that he must save himself for the fortuitous moment when that greatness presents itself. (It never does.) Like John Marcher, Fleda Vetch, in *The Spoils of Poynton,* holds herself in reserve for the moment when her true self will be recognized and appreciated. Unfortunately, whenever a promising moment comes, she refuses to seize it either because she cannot recognize it for what it is or because she prefers to wait for something else rather than compromise her precious scruples.

Perhaps the most arresting example of a Henry James character who takes perverse pleasure in renunciation is Catherine Sloper in *Washington Square.* Catherine is a plain and painfully shy heroine who falls madly in love with Morris Townsend, a handsome scoundrel who abandons her on the night of their elopement only to return years later, chastened by misfortune into wooing her back. But by then Catherine has been taught by her ruthless father how to be ruthless herself, and so, even though she might have a moment of happiness with a cad, she plots her revenge. At first she deliberately leads Morris on, even agreeing to run away with him again, but when he comes to fetch her, she refuses to admit him. Smiling at his suffering as he pounds on her door and begs her to let him in, she is now able to reject him once and for all and retreat into splendid spinsterhood, triumphant as a nun forsaking the world.

Karl Beckson talks of the "dark shadow of self-destruction" that fell across the decade of the nineties (xxxix). Self-destruction was to continue to cast its dark shadow across the century that followed and become a major motif in modern literature and a popular pastime among its practitioners. Names like F. Scott Fitzgerald, Malcolm Lowry, Delmore Schwartz, and Truman Capote come to mind as well as fictional characters such as Sebastian Flyte in Evelyn Waugh's *Brideshead Revisited,* Christopher Martin in William Golding's *Pincher Martin,* and Christopher Ransom in Jay McInerney's *Ransom.*

Sebastian Flyte is one of those tormented young men of the twenties who suffers the spiritual paralysis of a Prufrock, but Sebastian's anguish is compounded by sexual ambiguity and Catholic guilt. His hurting of others is never deliberate or malicious, but when he punishes himself it is in a self-indulgent way that suggests a decadent temperament. Sebastian languishes in his own corruption, especially when he flees to Morocco where, by allowing himself to be enslaved by a sleazy German named Kurt, he becomes a willing sacrifice to his own shame. Sick unto death, he puts himself at Kurt's mercy, eager to do Kurt's bidding, prepared to drag himself from his sickbed to fetch Kurt a drink or a cigarette, his bondage total and totally voluntary.

Christopher Martin is an actor whose ego is so enormous that he literally gets consumed by it. A sea accident strands him on a tiny coral rock in the middle of the Atlantic Ocean where, as he struggles to stay alive, he suffers hallucinations that force him to relive a lifetime of cruelty and carelessness motivated by monstrous vanity and ambition. The suffering he is forced to endure is intense. His body is soaked and freezing, and his hands turn to claws as he scrapes them fleshless against the razor-sharp reef. In the last stages of survival, he imagines that he has turned into an enormous, voracious mouth by which he himself will be devoured. To be devoured by one's own ego sounds very much like the decadent version of perishing by the sword one has lived by. Christopher Martin certainly gets the punishment he deserves, and when the experience turns out to be the nightmare of the drowning man, it also turns out to be Martin's salvation for he does get a second chance, and he accepts it thoroughly chastened. The rock has been his purgatory.

Jay McInerney's second novel, *Ransom,* is the story of a young American exile and athlete living in Japan and studying the martial arts. Christopher Ransom tortures his body into living up to the highest ideal of these Oriental skills, punishing his body unmercifully in his drive to be better than his Japanese adversaries. In the end he is killed by another American in a karate-style duel involving Oriental swords. This novel is an almost unparalleled chronicle of narcissistic masochism. It is perhaps symbolic, certainly fitting, that the story should culminate in the ritual slaying of the young hero who dies at the moment when his body has been tortured into reaching its peak.

While Henry James usually deals with subtler manifestations of the pursuit of pain, as in his tales of renunciation and masochistic self-sacrifice, in *The Turn of the Screw* he has written a story in which the giving and receiving of pain is the raw nerve on which the narrative is stretched. The story is narrated by an overwrought spinster who, after a sheltered childhood spent in a parsonage, becomes the governess of two precocious children who live with their housekeeper in the remote country house of Bly. Sharing the house with them, or so the governess would have us believe, are the ghosts of the former governess and her lover, Miss Jessel and Peter Quint, two evil people presumably intent on finishing the job they had begun of corrupting the children, Miles and Flora.

The narrator-governess, who has an overworked imagination but no real experience of life, convinces herself that she is being persecuted in her dealings with the children by the interference of the ghosts of Miss Jessel and Peter Quint and that she must suffer in order to save her charges. For she is quite convinced that Peter Quint has corrupted Miles while Miss Jessel has worked her sorcery on Flora. The result is that the governess, feeling victimized, all too eagerly assumes the role of avenging angel and decides that it is her painful duty to combat this monstrous villainy that she imagines surrounds her. We are never actually sure just what is fact and what is fancy in her story, but we do know that she drives Flora to hysteria and Miles to his death in the process of attempting to exorcise these alleged demons from the children's endangered souls. Meanwhile, her own anguish, as she is quick to remind us, is worse than anyone else's, and she rationalizes the extreme measures she feels she must take as necessary in her crusade against the powers of darkness.

There is good reason to believe that the governess is, if not demented, then certainly disturbed. Her upbringing was of a sort peculiar to the daughters of Victorian clergymen, a life so restricted that her only freedom was her imagination, which she has fueled to fever pitch with romantic fiction and frenzied dreams. Guilt over any thought that might be less than simon-pure can only be expiated by her discovery of a cause, in this case the salvation of the children. Once she sees clearly what her "duty" is, she is comfortable in the role of Victorian heroine, pure of heart and proud of spirit, her neuroses conveniently subsumed in the pursuit of a noble cause. That she must suffer goes without saying—as does the fact that others must suffer, too. Suffering, to her simple but overwrought mind, is good for the soul. In what is very nearly a parody of the suffering heroine tradition, James has exposed its decadent nerve.

In this novel, in addition to the pain suffered by the main character, there is the added element of the pain she inflicts on others. Whereas the sufferers in the mold of Dostoyevsky's underground man suffer much more pain than they inflict, in *The Turn of the Screw* the masochism of the central character is compounded by what is, in effect, her sadistic treatment of the children. In the case of the governess, this sadism is in the guise of compassion; it is not committed for the sake of pleasure—at least not consciously—but it is still not very far in practice, nor in effect, from the way Dr. Sloper treats his wretched daughter Catherine in *Washington Square*. It is not uncommon for those who feel obliged to punish others to take a certain satisfaction in redressing a grievance. In attempting to exorcise the children's demons, the governess reaches moments of intense feeling that strongly resemble ecstasy.

In *The Picture of Dorian Gray,* Dorian's mistreatment of others far exceeds any remorse he may feel. In fact, it is not until near the end of the story that Dorian begins to experience the self-loathing that hastens his end. Even so, instead of reforming him, this self-loathing only pushes him more deeply into evil behavior. Dorian's most vile crime is undoubtedly his cruel treatment of Basil Hallward, the artist who, victimized by his own adoration of Dorian, painted the portrait that captured Dorian's very soul. Ever since he first noticed an alteration in the portrait, Dorian has refused to let anyone see it. Now, near the end of his life, when the picture betrays what his beauty belies, Dorian decides to show Hallward the painting in all its ugliness. "You have chattered enough about corruption," he says to Hallward. "Now you shall look on it face to face." Wilde says that "there was the madness of pride in every word he uttered. He stamped his foot upon the ground in his boyish insolent manner. He felt a terrible joy at the thought that someone else was to share his secret, and that the man who had painted the portrait that was the origin of all his shame was to be burdened for the rest of his life with the hideous memory of what he had done" (312).

Atrocious as it is, the murder of Basil Hallward after he has seen the picture is something of an anticlimax after what Dorian has done to Hallward's soul. In a way, killing him is almost an act of mercy, for he has already killed Hallward spiritually. Dorian's murder of Hallward is his only acknowledged act of deliberate physical violence, and although it cannot be excused, it could be looked upon as the tragic end towards which Hallward's life had inevitably been moving. If it is true as Wilde says in "The Ballad of Reading Gaol" that we all kill the thing we love, then it may also be true that the thing we love can just as easily kill us.

It is possible that Dorian's most diabolical act of calculated cruelty, worse in its consequences than murder, is his blackmailing of Alan Campbell into disposing of Hallward's body. We can only guess at the secret of Campbell's degradation, but we have no doubt about who was behind it. All we know is that whatever it was, it is enough to persuade Campbell to carry out the abominable task and then to drive him to take his own life.

As his wicked life grows more loathsome and he begins to worry a bit about what will happen to him, Dorian inevitably gets around to the masochistic pleasure of remorse. He certainly has much to regret as he looks back on his life and sees how it has been spent, but it is the phony regret of the sinner who has simply grown tired of his sins. When Lord Henry says, "There is no one who would not be delighted to change places with you," Dorian sighs and says, "There is no one with whom I would not change places, Harry" (368). He is not sorry for what he has done; he is only sorry that the fun has gone out of it.

Fate itself is often viewed as the sadist who tortures those who either want too much and cannot get it or get too much and no longer want it. Much of Dorian's self-pity has to do with the fact that he has exhausted every pleasure possible and has become "sick with that ennui, that terrible *tædium vitæ,* that comes on those to whom life denies nothing" (303). Karl Beckson suggests that the weariness of the decadent is more likely to be an affectation, a "mark of sophistication and moral superiority" born of his quest for new and preferably abnormal experiences (xxx).

In contemporary literature, one of the most disturbing examples of ennui leading to new and abnormal experiences, experiences which turn morbidly sadomasochistic, is to be found in Ian McEwan's 1981 novella, *The Comfort of Strangers.* Called by one reviewer "a sadomasochistic *Death in Venice,*" this short novel relates the macabre story of two couples whose encounter one summer in Venice becomes a nightmare of abnormal experiences. Colin and Mary, married (but not to each other), are together in Venice on an extended stay that has degenerated into an effort to endure ennui. They float through their days in a trance, doing little but taking long naps, fussing endlessly over their appearance, and going through the daily routine of drinks and dinner and aimless walks. It is obvious that they are bored with each other but feel almost powerless to escape the vacuum into which they have slipped. Then they encounter Robert, a sinister character who comes upon them on one of their walks and invites them to a seedy little bar that seems to cater to men. Colin and Mary are so detached from any previous moorings, so bereft of any self-sufficiency, that they are attracted to Robert like moths to a flame.

Without admitting it to each other—or even to themselves—they enjoy the excitement of the sense of adventure, even danger, that Robert offers. Later they meet Robert's wife, Caroline, a woman who boasts about the pain she has suffered at the hands of her sadistic husband. She admits that she has grown to enjoy the abuse, not the pain itself but, as she puts it, "the fact of the pain, of being helpless before it, and being reduced to nothing by it. It's pain in a particular context," she explains, "being punished and therefore being guilty. We both liked what was happening. I was ashamed of myself, and before I knew it, my shame too was a source of pleasure. . . . I was terrified," she adds, "but the terror and the pleasure were all one."

Having nothing in her earlier experience to be ashamed of, Caroline finds that this lack of guilt is itself a source of shame. She also finds that accepting punishment for sins she never committed is a source of even greater shame—and thus of greater pleasure. "Instead of saying loving things into my ear, he whispered pure hatred," she tells Mary, "and though I was sick with humiliation, I thrilled to the point of passing out. I didn't doubt Robert's hatred for me. It wasn't theater. He made love to me out of deep loathing, and I couldn't resist. I loved being punished" (122). It is an ingenious spiral which turns nasty when the circle must widen to feed tastes grown jaded.

So enthralled do Colin and Mary become that even when they know they should stay away, they are drawn irresistibly to return to Robert and Caroline's villa. Too late they realize that they have been singled out by this weird couple precisely because they look like people desperate for anything to fill the void their lives have become. Robert operates in a way reminiscent of Cipolla in Thomas Mann's "Mario and the Magician," the hypnotist whose easiest victims are those who put up no positive resistance. Eventually, he murders Colin in a ritual in which Caroline takes part and which Mary, drugged, is forced to watch. By the time Mary comes to her senses, Robert and Caroline have left without a trace. In this probing study of the psychology of pain, McEwan suggests that the giving and receiving of pain may be one remedy for the absence of feeling that has become a commonplace modern malaise. Even more disturbing, perhaps, is the suggestion that some people, like Caroline, suffer from an absence of suffering and must seek out pain to satisfy a curious craving for shame and humiliation.

The most graphic analysis of sadomasochism in all of modern literature is to be found in Kafka's "In the Penal Colony." In this chilling short story, Kafka explores what might be called the politics of pain. The clinical setting, the laboratory atmosphere, the frightening reasonableness of its presentation make this the ultimate nightmare of modern times. Here punishment is raised to a fine art, refined far beyond the imaginative but crude instruments of torture that were the pride of the Spanish Inquisition. In the penal colony in which the story takes place, those condemned to die must first submit to twelve hours of the most exquisite torture inflicted by a machine specifically designed for this purpose. Unlike the thumb screws and the rack, whose purpose was to save a soul by torturing a heretic into confession, this machine exists solely for its own sake; and in order for the machine to be refined and tested, it must have bodies to practice on.

This instrument of torture looks something like a giant rotisserie on which a naked victim slowly revolves as sharp needles attached to a glass harrow etch the name of the crime onto his skin. Much care is taken to see that only the surface of the skin is pricked and that the calligraphy is properly elaborate. There is also an ingenious drainage system for washing away the blood so that the writing can be seen by those who enjoy watching the machine perform its function. The victims, who do not know what their crime is until they comprehend what is being written upon their bodies, are said to experience a

euphoric exaltation at the end of the sixth hour, at which time they understand the nature of their crimes and the justice of their punishment. At the end
of this story, when the machine begins to break down and its caretaker realizes
that its day is over, he throws himself onto the machine and dies horribly as it
malfunctions and impales his body on a hundred needles.

Ernst Pawel says that this story was the result of "an outburst of self-hatred,
sadism, and visionary rage so savage that in its time most readers reacted with
either disgust or defensive indifference" (327). "In the Penal Colony" was apparently inspired by *Le Jardin des Supplices,* (1899), a sensational novel by Oc-
tave Mirbeau, which was banned when it first appeared in German. Pawel says
that it is difficult to account for the profound impression Mirbeau's "ornate
decadence" made on Kafka without assuming that the book's graphic sadism
provoked a sympathetic response somewhere deep in Kafka's unconscious
(327–328). It is known that Kafka wrote this short story after receiving a dis-
tressing letter from a former mistress, and that the letter opened old wounds.
"The pain it caused, the pain it made him want to inflict on himself," says
Pawel, "erupted in a vision of violence stripped of all its extrinsic components,
the very essence of evil in its naked, terrifying banality" (328).

The decadence in this story has several facets. One of them is the scientific
objectivity, the professional detachment on the part of the officer as he carefully explains how the machine works and then fusses over its operation as it
goes about its job of cutting into the flesh of its helpless victim. Another facet
is the willingness with which the officer sacrifices himself to the machine as it
scratches "Be Just" on his body, apparently a sign that he feels guilty about his
inability to make the machine a perfect instrument of "justice." Yet another
facet of decadence is the eagerness of the condemned man, once he is freed
after the machine breaks down, to take part in the torture and execution of the
officer who has replaced him on the machine's bed, not at all out of revenge
but simply out of callous curiosity.

Jean-Baptiste Grenouille, the main character in Patrick Süskind's *Perfume,* is a
more recent example in modern literature of the extremes to which self-love
and self-loathing can lead one. Grenouille begins by despising himself because
he is ugly and deformed and thus an object of derision. But once he realizes
the genius he has for perfumes, he comes to think of himself as some kind of
god. The conflict between these extremes comes to a climax at the end of the
novel when, after eliciting adoration from the mob that originally came to see
him dismembered, he escapes to Paris where, in total desperation, he provokes
his own assassination, not just by dismemberment but by cannibalism.

After the pandemonium his perfume created at the site of the execution,
Grenouille knows that he has reached the limit of his strange genius, and he
now finds himself miserable and alone. He possesses the power to enslave
mankind in a frenzy of love, but what bothers him is that he is unable to smell
his own odor while the scent he concocts has the power to make others fall at

his feet in veneration. He finally concludes that appearing before the world as a god means nothing at all to him if he is incapable of knowing his own smell and, therefore, incapable of knowing who he is. If that is the case, he thinks, then "to hell with it, with the world, with himself, with his perfume" (306).

In despair, he wanders about Paris until he comes upon a paupers' graveyard where the derelicts who dig the graves and bury the corpses work at night when the air is cooler and the stench less odious. Alone among these derelicts, he pauses, unstops a bottle, and sprinkles himself with its contents, and suddenly he is "bathed in beauty like blazing fire." The crowd hesitates momentarily, then is irresistibly drawn to this man who comes to them as an angel exuding an allure too potent to resist (if they even cared to), for so strong is this force that it pulls them straight to him like a strong tide that drags the hapless swimmer to the bottom of the sea.

At first the crowd falls back in amazement, but once their surprise has abated, the derelicts form a circle around him, which grows smaller and smaller until the circle cannot contain them all, and they begin to push and shove and elbow their way to the center, each trying to get the closest to him. All at once, as the last inhibition collapses, the circle collapses with it, and the derelicts overwhelm him, forcing him to the ground in their frenzied attempt to tear from him something for themselves. They rip the clothing from his body and the hair from his head as they sink their teeth and their claws into his flesh, attacking him "like hyenas" (309).

Unable to dismember him by hand, they resort to knives and axes and cleavers, "thrusting and slicing . . . hacking and crushing the bones" (309). It is not long before they have divided him into "thirty pieces, and every animal in the pack snatch[es] a piece for itself, and then, driven by voluptuous lust, drop[s] back to devour it." Within half an hour, Grenouille has ceased to exist, and on the faces of the cannibals there is now "a delicate, virginal glow of happiness" (309).

The ugly eroticism of the orgy scene with its equal measure of pleasure and pain is the figment of a de Sade fantasy. And Grenouille's ritual death, a grotesque parody of the eucharist, is a masochistic fantasy in which, by luring others to cannibalize him, he gets them to perform, with his blessing, the ultimate act of indecency and abasement. In much the same way, Sebastian, in Tennessee Williams's *Suddenly Last Summer*, deliberately entices the starving children on the beach in Spain into overwhelming him and devouring his flesh in a ritual of voluntary degradation.

The decadent recluse intent on suffering appears in a new guise in Paul Auster's *The New York Trilogy*, three highly original novels published in the mid-1980s. Each novel is totally different from the others in terms of time frame and circumstances, but all three have in common a central character whose paranoia drives him to inhabit a solitary nightmare even while the city of New York surrounds him. The Kafkaesque quality of Auster's stories can be seen in *Ghosts,* the second novel in the trilogy, in which Auster uses colors for the names of characters and places; and while he is as straightforward as Kafka in his storytelling, such a device as using colors for names gives an unreal quality to the story which belies its utter clarity.

In *Ghosts* the main character is a man named Blue who is a student of Brown and who has been hired by White to spy on Black. From a rented room on Orange Street, Blue keeps watch out his window, making notes about his subject, who sits across the street in another rented room, staring out *his* window. Weeks go by and nothing happens, yet Blue, instead of giving up, continues to file his reports (or nonreports). Meanwhile, he patiently waits and watches. Nothing will induce him to leave his room. In fact, for a long time the thought never enters his mind. Meanwhile, he concocts one scenario after another to explain who Black is and what he may be up to. Just as Kafka's characters never know why things happen to them, Blue has not been told why he has been given this assignment or what he is supposed to be on the lookout for.

The life Blue lives is one of total isolation, his only activity being the non-activity of staring out the window at a figure who, when he is not writing at his desk, is staring back. What makes this an interesting new twist on deca-dent self-punishment is that while Blue accepts this tedious assignment as something he deserves, he seems to have reached a point beyond, say, the ago-nizing guilt of Josef K. in *The Trial,* to a place where there is no question of one's guilt, only of the nature of one's punishment. There are echoes in this novel of Dostoyevsky's underground man. Blue, for instance, has not been in touch with his fiancée for several months, not even by telephone. One day, when he finally ventures out of his room, he happens to see her walking down the street on the arm of another man. When she in turn sees him, she immedi-ately attacks him, pounding him on the chest and screaming at him. He ac-cepts her anger and her punishment, but he blames White who has set him up and then abandoned him, so he stakes out the post office box where White collects his mail. But his waiting, which goes on for days, is, of course, in vain.

Self-induced humiliations and pointless recriminations continue through-out the novel which ends with Blue killing Black, stealing his manuscript, and returning to his own room to read it. Then he stands up, puts on his hat, and walks out the door. After that, says the author, we know nothing. At least Blue staked out his quarry in the comfort of a hotel room. His counterpart, the enigmatic Quinn of *City of Glass,* spends months in a New York alley, looking at the slice of sky between the buildings, not really sure what he is doing there.

There is a final dimension to decadent suffering that goes beyond the tor-ment that fictional characters may invite or inflict or that artists may willingly submit to, and that is the deliberate torturing of the audience. The desire to engage the audience in the thrill of suspense by placing characters in distress-ing circumstances has always been a staple of the art of storytelling, but even in the most terrifying of Gothic horror stories, there has always been enough distance between reader and story to allow the reader to shrug off any discomfort with a shudder of horrified delight. The reason for this is probably, as Jane Austen made clear in her Gothic parody, *Northanger Abbey,* that there is little physical realism and even less psychological realism in traditional Gothic fiction. However, beginning with Poe, an element of psychological realism appeared in the horror story that made the emotional responses of the characters adhere to the consciousness of the readers in a way that was not at all easy to shrug off. It is one thing for a stock villain to torture a stock maiden; it is quite another for a seemingly dutiful husband to sink an axe into his wife's brain in a fit or rage and then try to conceal her body behind a brick wall. The former speaks to a libidinous fantasy that is not entirely unpleasant; the latter is all too close to the terrors of everyday reality—and to the repressed diabolism in all of us—to be anything but disquieting.

It is this shock of recognition that both attracts and repels us, and it has been an enduring—and enormously popular—ingredient in fiction for nearly two centuries. The artist who writes with the purpose of making his readers writhe in fascinated horror is going beyond the presentation of sadism to the practice of it. Dostoyevsky's underground man is such an accurate portrayal of a masochistic paranoid personality that any reader who identifies with him may feel as if his own soul has been laid embarrassingly bare. When Henry James forces us to share the very real agony of the governess in *The Turn of the Screw*, he torments us by refusing to oblige us with easy answers to the mystery. In fact, James boasted in his preface to this novella that he considered it "a piece of ingenuity pure and simple, of cold artistic calculation, an *amusette* to catch those not easily caught." And then, after pausing to admit that there is little fun in capturing the "merely witless," he identifies his intended audience as "the jaded, the disillusioned, the fastidious," a perfect description of a decadent (*Art,* 172).

Early in this century it was Franz Kafka who gave us nightmares that did not disappear in the light of day. More recently it is Stephen King who has drawn us into the narrative as fellow sufferers. King has himself long suffered the fate of the enormously popular author whose success automatically alienates the critics. Those who have not read him are quick to call him vulgar and cheap, an exploiter, a charlatan, a fraud. Whatever he is, he knows how to tell a story. He is exuberantly imaginative and—something too often ignored or overlooked—marvelously comic. It is a sign of his virtuosity and his confidence that he can say something funny at a gripping moment in the story and still manage to send chills down the spine. It is his own way, of course, of knocking at Macbeth's gate.

In a review of a King novel in *The New York Times,* Christopher Lehmann-Haupt made a remark that sums up the response of most intelligent readers who feel guilty about their taste for King: "Anybody who can make me read a book called *The Tommyknockers* has to be some kind of genius." Unfortunately, *The Tommyknockers* is typical of a side of King that sprawls and seems out of control, a side that raises the suspicion that he knows he can get away with anything, for it mixes horror and humor in equal measure. But it is precisely because he *can* get away with anything that he even gets away with making fun of his readers for letting him do it. This is the trick he pulls off so adroitly in *Misery,* one of his most intense, most controlled, most complex, and most challenging novels.

Misery is King's extraordinary commentary on the vicissitudes of an enormously popular writer at the mercy of his audience. The book's writer-narrator, Paul Sheldon, is persecuted beyond belief by a deranged fan of his into whose clutches he falls after she has "rescued" him from an automobile accident in a remote mountain region of Colorado. Paul Sheldon (as in Sidney) is the author of a series of prodigiously popular historical novels featuring a bewitching heroine named Misery Chastaine. Annie Wilkes, the deranged fan, has read every one of them, many times over, and it is only because she recognizes Sheldon as the author that she bothers to take his broken body back to her cottage and nurse him back to health. Actually, he desperately needs hospitalization and surgery, which means that her "nursing" itself has a sadistic twist to it.

What thrills her now is that she will be able to read the next Misery book just as it comes out of the typewriter. The problem is that in his last Misery novel, Paul killed off his heroine and vowed never to write another piece of trash again. He soon realizes, however, that, like Scheherazade, his only way of staying alive is to humor Annie Wilkes and so, on her orders, he "resurrects" Misery and begins another sequel. Annie may be crazy, but she is not stupid, and when Paul tries to get away with a plot that does not ring true, she flies into a psychotic rage. Forced, therefore, to write a book she will accept, Paul finds himself reluctantly caught up in the machinations of the sort of story he thinks he loathes but which he writes so well. It may be a horrible position for Paul Sheldon to be in, but it is also a very uncomfortable position for his readers to be in, knowing that the writer whose book they are engrossed in is ridiculing them for reading it and for forcing the writer to go on writing books they love but which he purports to hate. To be lumped in with Annie Wilkes and still love every minute of the story (including the sample "Misery" chapters which King throws in!) is to participate in a sadomasochistic duet between author and reader of unparalleled humiliation.

"Sometimes I think that the artistic life is a long and lovely suicide, and am not sorry that it is so," Oscar Wilde once remarked to his friend Harry Marillier (Ellmann, 270). When Annie Wilkes forces Paul to burn the only copy of his one serious novel, to him it is an act of suicide, for he is destroying a part of himself that is irretrievable. And when he surrenders to her demands, after contemplating suicide, he does it with a feeling of yielding up another pound of flesh. The self-loathing, the spite, the shame, the degradation—

these are ingredients King has exploited in every novel beginning with *Carrie,* and they are what give his novels their decadent overtones.

In the same way that they are prone to exaggerate their virtues, decadents are likely to overrate their vices. Thus, while smugness may tempt them to taunt others, often quite mercilessly, remorse goads them to torment themselves with equal fury. By flaunting society's fashionable vices, they are scorned as depraved, but their flaunting is mere mockery, a means of bringing disapproval down about their heads the way a saintly person courts abuse by his pious behavior. In a way they are much like the religious flagellants who flogged themselves in a frenzied attempt to exorcise their own evil—and thus the world's. The difference is that the decadent's sense of worthlessness is like the itch of a missing limb, an itch no scratch can relieve. Within them they sense the presence of a moral imperative they find embarrassing because it would seem to be in direct contradiction to the amorality—if not, indeed, the immorality—of the pose they take such pains to strike. The irony of the situation is anathema to the decadent temperament and renders it peculiarly susceptible to radical remedies.

Chapter 8:

The Heel of Achilles

Better the rule of One, whom all obey,
Than to let clamorous demagogues betray
Our freedom with the kiss of anarchy.
                    Oscar Wilde, "Libertatis Sacra Fames"

There is a curious naiveté in the decadent temperament that is as disturbing as it is surprising. It is most apt to reveal itself at that point where self-love and self-loathing intersect and render one vulnerable to the lure of persons or systems that hold out promises of power. One would think that decadents could resist any attempt to enlist their sympathies, that they would be the last to forfeit their independence, but there are certain circumstances under which their defenses against exploitation are easily penetrated. While decadents may be good at resisting vulgar attempts at recruitment from forces they deplore, they are not good at resisting those subtler temptations that masquerade as projections of their own pride. They are impatient with those who are slow to acknowledge their superiority, and eager to embrace those who do. Thus, any system that flatters their pride under the guise of praising their judgment is attractive to them, for, like Caesar, they are most flattered when they are told that they hate flatterers.

Decadents are, in a word, gullible. Obsessed with themselves and skeptical of all systems, they live inside a self-made image, a soft and fragile shell which cracks under the pressures of loneliness and dread. Since decadence is a philosophy and not a faith, there is nothing at its core to help its disciples combat loneliness or defend themselves against dread. Thus they become vulnerable, particularly to the hypnotic allure of power, be it social, religious, or political.

The source of this vulnerability has been traced to an agitated mental condition that manifested itself during the late nineteenth century in Europe, particularly among decadent artists. In *The Decadent Imagination: 1880–1900,* Jean Pierrot paints a vivid portrait of this prototypical decadent as an unbalanced being in whom "an excessive delicacy of the sensibility and the nerves, plus a hypertrophied critical intelligence, takes its revenge by destroying the faculty of will and the desire to act." The result is an "impotence of the will" made even worse by the burden of the vast history he has inherited and the knowledge that this cultural legacy is one fraught with contradictions (52).

When he looks back upon centuries of cultural experimentation and rejection, of customs and beliefs passionately adopted and just as passionately rejected, says Pierrot, the decadent artist is torn by anguish and uncertainty and doubt, "and the naive faith of former ages is succeeded by an inevitable and profound skepticism." This skepticism, according to Pierrot, results first in dilettantism, "which consists in a refusal, and an incapacity, to take up any definitive moral or intellectual stance, a sort of Don Juanism of the intellect," and second in cosmopolitanism, "which makes the artist into a being forever deprived of roots, incapable of integrating himself into any national collectivity" (52).

Deprived of the will to resist, decadents are as defenseless against the magnetism of power as Mario, in "Mario and the Magician," is against hypnotism. In Mann's short story, young Mario is struggling in vain to prevent himself from being hypnotized by the traveling magician who is entertaining the inhabitants of a small Italian village. Mario keeps telling himself that he will not surrender, but the harder he struggles, the more vulnerable he becomes until finally, against his will, he succumbs. As we saw earlier, Mann makes it clear that people who try to resist hypnosis are often the most susceptible to it because they think only negatively and thus create a void which any charlatan is invited to fill. To resist hypnosis, it is necessary to fill that void with something positive that will obstruct the influence of the hypnotist. In this story, which takes place during the dictatorship of Mussolini, Mann shows how easy it is for people to be taken in by political hypnosis, in this case fascism. Unless they resist it with some counter ideology of their own, they have no defense against its mesmerizing logic.

This, then, is precisely the moral vacuum which decadent naiveté creates, and it has been the bane of romantic temperaments from the followers of Rousseau to Ken Kesey's merry pranksters and beyond. They delude themselves into believing that they have arrived at their beliefs entirely on their own and that it is sheer coincidence that others have come to similar beliefs on their own, too. They are now ready to join with their own kind in a sort of mutual dissimulation society best described as "individual togetherness," a paradox that leaves those who are taken in by it wide open to its more sinister allures.

Decadents are particularly susceptible to this delusion. Sure of themselves but unsure of everything else, they fall back on their prejudices, incapable of seeing that their prejudices are unreliable illusions that the crafty know how to exploit. This is why so many sensitive temperaments in this century have succumbed to the seductions of extreme political ideologies and esoteric religions. George Bernard Shaw's letters, for example, reveal him as, in one critic's terms, a "fool of the new totalitarians" who called Adolf Hitler a "'wonderful preacher of everything that is right and best in Toryism'" and Joseph Stalin the "'greatest living statesman'" (Kanfer, 87). Shaw's plays are political and social tracts disguised—brilliantly, to be sure—as comedies, and the ideologies to be found in plays like *Man and Superman, Major Barbara, The Apple Cart,* and *Back to Methuselah* bear a disconcerting resemblance to those satirized by Huxley and Orwell as totalitarian. Huxley and Orwell, of course, succumbed to their own ideological weaknesses, Huxley to the worship of Ramakrishna, Orwell to liberal socialism. However, in their soberer moments these men wrote two of the century's most "Kafkaesque" nightmares of political extremism, *Brave New World* and *1984,* both of which can be read as decadent fantasies of power and control.

Shaw's reputation as a socialist obscures the naiveté of his politics by making him sound like someone passionately interested in social reform. The truth is that his idea of reforming British society sprang from a belief in the Life Force that, "if human stupidity permitted," says Anthony Burgess, "would in time produce supermen and superwomen" (*Atlantic,* 94). His idea of reforming British taste took the form of theatrical satire that owes more to Wilde than to Ibsen, says Burgess, arguing that Shaw "originated few ideas" and that his greatest invention was himself. Burgess comments on Shaw's "monster ego," calling it a "farcical mask" that, he says, concealed Shaw's altruism.

This is not hard to believe, since, altruism, as we know, is just as likely to be a product of a patronizing sentimentality activated by a "monster ego" as an expression of genuine humanitarian compassion. Des Esseintes is an altruist to the extent that he cares enough about society to let its inanities preoccupy him, and it is in such intense preoccupation that the spirit of reform germinates. Burgess tells us that Shaw was "overweening only to shock," that he said he despised Shakespeare only to whip "thoughtless bardolators," that he was a doubter and a sufferer, "unafraid to look absurd since absurdity was a door to self-understanding and even intellectual progress. And if GBS was heartless," says Burgess, "Bernard Shaw wept for the wrongs and fatuities of the world" (94). Decadence cast a long shadow over both personalities.

D.H. Lawrence's politics have puzzled most critics if only because his public statements often seemed to contradict his fictional ones. On the one hand, he might rage against the Germans and wish to battle them single-handed, but on the other hand he could write admiringly of them at a time when their behavior was creating consternation among more level-headed observers. In the opinion of literary historian Robert Adams, Lawrence's *Kangaroo* is "a thinly disguised fascist tract," one, he says, that makes "very heavy reading these days" (*Land*, 482). Certainly the political party led by Benjamin Cooley in that novel, the party that Richard Lovat Somers, the character based on Lawrence, is drawn to is an obvious blend of fascism and Lawrence's famous doctrine of "blood-consciousness," his version of Shaw's Life Force. Incidentally, it was Lawrence whose encouragement to Huxley to look for spiritual values when in despair led Huxley to dabble in the occult and to experiment with drugs along the path to Ramakrishna.

There is a passivity to decadent naiveté that renders decadents susceptible to lotusland utopias. Like Ulysses, they hardly notice how they got where they are and are soon unable to resist whatever temptations are present. Gustav Aschenbach, after a lifetime of rigid self-discipline, succumbs with little resistance to the lure of the lotus when he travels to Venice. Even though he had not consciously planned to spend his vacation in Venice, the suspicion that he would end up there had always hovered just below the surface of his consciousness. On his way by boat to Venice, "alert for the first glimpse of the coast," he is overpowered by a melancholy lethargy and by mingled emotions which render him "easily susceptible to a prescience already shaped within him." At this point he wonders if "a new preoccupation, some late adventure of the feelings could still be in store for the idle traveller" (452).

Aschenbach is ripe for surrender. He has gradually loosened the reigns on his self-control and become increasingly reckless. "He who is beside himself revolts at the idea of self-possession," says Mann (490). Later, trapped in a coffin-like gondola and completely at the mercy of a despotic gondolier, Aschenbach is surprised to find that he is curiously untroubled by what would otherwise be a threatening situation. "The thought passed dreamily through [his] brain that perhaps he had fallen into the clutches of a criminal; it had not power to rouse him to action" (455). Lacking self-possession, he has no defenses against moral erosion and will soon, in fact, actively court it.

Once a man like Aschenbach lets go, a man who has long prided himself on total objectivity and utter detachment, he neither tries, nor even wants, to regain that detachment. He is like a swimmer caught in a current that is propelling him away from safety and quite content to drift, ready to embrace whatever fate the current may be carrying him toward. As Aschenbach feels pulled inexorably into the maelstrom of obsession and disease, he is increasingly loath to halt his descent. He reaches the point where "the thought of returning home, returning to reason, self-mastery, an ordered existence, to the old life of effort . . . made him wince with a revulsion that was like physical nausea." This is one reason he decides to remain silent about the plague, even if it means risking the lives of Tadzio and his family.

To their own surprise, decadents may find themselves susceptible to influences they thought they had thoroughly avoided when they were first exposed to them. This is the case with Des Esseintes who boasts that the conditioning to which he had been subject at the Jesuit school he attended as a young man has been totally without effect. He was much too inquisitive to take anything on authority and much too disputatious to accept anything on faith. Once he leaves school, his skepticism grows as he encounters narrow-minded intolerance among the laity and ignorance and uncouthness among the clergy. However, in his solitude, he begins to wonder if he has really remained immune to the teachings of his masters, "whether the seed which had fallen on apparently barren ground was not showing signs of germinating" (86).

For a period of several days he finds himself strangely torn, vacillating between intense moments of belief and tortured moments of renewed doubt and uneasiness. He knows he could never feel "the humility and contrition of a true Christian" or experience grace. He has no hunger for the "mortification and prayer" necessary for conversion, nor does he feel the desire to invoke a God "whose mercy struck him as extremely problematical" (86–87). Yet the pull of the Church remains, and the only way Des Esseintes can rationalize this irrational attraction is to attribute it to the fact that "the Church was the only body to have preserved the art of past centuries, the lost beauty of the ages" (87). And even though he continues to regard the Christian religion as a "superb legend, a magnificent imposture" and to remind himself of all his arguments against it, he finds that his skepticism is beginning to crack. But rather than surrender to the Church, Des Esseintes turns to a substitute, in this case Schopenhauer who, in his opinion, comes nearer to the truth. Thus, a part of the psychology of decadent vulnerability is the need for an alternative to religion, preferably an alternative with all of religion's power to command total subservience.

Even Dorian Gray secretly desires to be "something more than a mere *arbiter elegantiarum*," more than a dandy who is fit only to give advice on "the wearing of a jewel, or the knotting of a necktie, or the conduct of a cane." He wants more, and what he wants is "to elaborate some new scheme of life that would have its reasoned philosophy and its ordered principles, and find in the spiritualizing of the senses its highest realization" (285). It is just this kind of fuzzy romanticism that tempts decadents to sympathize with ideologues whose philosophies seem reasoned and whose principles appear to be ordered, ideologues who promise the spiritualizing of the senses as their highest priority. The next step is to assist them in imposing their reason and their order on the unwilling whose senses are unworthy of spiritualization. Although such utopian dreams may appear to be progressive, they are usually quite reactionary in that they can only be realized in a society where freedom is curtailed, equality ignored, and rule of an elite—an allegedly enlightened elite—absolute.

Claude Ryals points out that romanticism in literature is the equivalent of liberalism in politics, whereas decadence is "highly conservative, if not outright reactionary. The decadent of the nineties," he says, "thought of his era not as the beginning of a new way of life, as the romantics had done, but as the culmination of the past" (90). It is not really surprising to find this reactionary tendency within the decadent temperament. After all, anyone convinced that the best is behind and that the world is in decline is bound to prefer a system that preserves what is in place to a system that threatens to make alarming changes.

There is also a side to the reactionary that actually prefers the excitement of unresolved dilemmas to the tedium of resolution. In *Dorian Gray,* Dorian recounts a favorite story of Lord Henry's having to do with a philanthropist who spent twenty years in an attempt to redress some grievance or other and who, when at last he succeeded, felt extremely disappointed. "He had absolutely nothing to do," says Dorian, "almost died of ennui, and became a confirmed misanthrope" (263). A taste for lost or hopeless causes is really nothing more than a faded legacy of romanticism, the difference being that the romantics thought they could make a difference, could really change things, whereas the decadents think that any change can only be for the worse. One would think that resistance to change would make decadents politically conservative. However, their willingness to unload the burden of social responsibility onto the government would put decadents squarely in the liberal camp. The truth is that their ambivalence makes them hard to pin down. To swim consistently against the tide means that they have to reverse direction each time the tide changes.

When they do get involved, decadents are drawn to systems that offer clear and firm control, systems that seem free of mundane politicking, systems that they think have more respect for the "oligarchy of the artist." Such evanescent aspirations toward an autocratic system often take shape under the influence of those whose wealth and power the decadent artist finds intoxicating. The appeal is particularly strong when wealth and power bear the legitimacy of aristocratic tradition. Thomas Mann makes the observation in *Death in Venice* that there is an innate tendency in the nature of such artists "to single out aristocratic pretensions and pay them homage" (458). The very ones who feel they owe nothing to the many are all too eager to pledge their fealty to the few whom they consider superior and into whose company they hope to be welcomed.

Isak Dinesen is modern literature's most obvious example of the artist who prefers the excitement and risk of an aristocratic hierarchy to the dull and dubious comforts of a democracy. Born into a middle-class family, she came to despise the bourgeoisie to the point of marrying an aristocrat she did not love simply to escape a bourgeois life and acquire the title of Baroness Blixen, a title she clung to in spite of divorce and scandal. She favored the rule of an enlightened nobility and undoubtedly counted herself among those favored few who knew how to rule.

As a plantation owner in Africa, Dinesen played the roles of feudal aristocrat, benevolent despot, and ruler by divine right, all according to the highest code of honor. Because she understood what true nobility was she alone among the colonials in Kenya was able to appreciate the true nobility of the native Africans, and her respect for their natural aristocracy was genuine. There is a kind of ingenuousness about her belief that she had a vocation to rule, but in her case, there seems to have been more than a grain of truth to it.

In discussing Dinesen's aristocratic pretensions, Eric Johannesson, in *The World of Isak Dinesen,* suggests that the aristocrat sees life as a game of chess in which the important thing is to play according to the rules. The aristocrat, with his loyalty to rules, becomes, then, an esthetic rather than a moral type, according to Johannesson (97). He is loyal to a code because codes "confer value on human life by disguising its essential and fundamental emptiness. They preserve the mystery which is no mystery. The aristocratic code," says Johannesson, "is a tacit agreement among civilized individuals to preserve the beauty and grace of life by making it into an elegant game" (99).

In recounting how Dinesen was forced to forsake the feudal society she had thrived on in Africa for the bleakness of Denmark in the early years of the depression, Donald Hannah characterizes her as "an aristocrat in exile from a world that no longer even existed" (*Isak,* 66). Her brother Thomas called her a "reactionary" (Thurman, 172), and Aage Henriksen claimed that "she suffered from a craving for power in spite of her generosity" (Thurman, 370). In her biography of Dinesen, Judith Thurman says that Dinesen's political views were subject to erratic swings, moving in opposition to the current fashion. But "the one fixed point," says Thurman, "was her aversion to all things middle class" (173).

As a young girl Dinesen had revered the French Revolution, but later she spoke of radicals as "scarcely human," lamenting the decline of manners and privilege and culture and the blurring of old class distinctions. "The impulse to defend her independence—to set herself apart from the herd, to be unique—remain[ed] constant while her values change[d]," says Thurman. "When the consensus was conservative, prudish, and patriarchal, she was radical, liberated, and modern. As it became more liberal—then Marxist, in postwar Denmark—she took it upon herself to represent the *ancien régime,* made up 'decadent' and fantastic stories about her past, and took great glee in shocking people with her 'aristocratic pronouncements'" (173).

This ambivalence is best expressed—and resolved—in Dinesen's "Sorrow-Acre," a tale set in the late eighteenth century at the time when revolutionary democratic principles were sweeping Europe and America. At an estate in Jutland, Adam, a young man infected with the new liberalism, comes in conflict with his uncle, the lord of the manor, who is the embodiment of the aristocratic code. The son of one of his tenants has been found guilty of barn burning and sent to jail, and to earn his release Anne-Marie, the boy's mother, offers to mow a field of rye between sunrise and sundown, a feat that ordinarily requires the labor of three men. The mother succeeds, and her son is released, but she dies of exhaustion at the moment she finishes the task. The whole idea outrages the liberal young nephew at first, but gradually he comes to understand his uncle's point: The old lord has given Anne-Marie his word; the two of them have made a pact. To stop her before she finishes would be to break the pact, violate the code, and thus make a mockery of the old woman's efforts.

Even though the nephew comes to accept his uncle's aristocratic philosophy, it is Adam's liberal views that have come to prevail in western culture in the two hundred years since then. And instead of enduring as an ideal, the code of the aristocrat has become subversive, a threat to democracy, and thereby a decadent stance. Johannesson calls this code a "luxury which only aristocrats can afford" (104). It is also one that only decadents can appreciate, one might add.

Truman Capote appreciated it. As Gerald Clarke points out, Capote looked upon people of "power and achievement," people who knew the difference between "what was stylish and what was merely expensive," the way "the Greeks looked upon their gods, with mingled awe and envy." It was Capote's belief that money did more than simply enlarge their lives; "it also excused them from the ordinary rules of behavior—or, indeed, any rules at all," he thought. These people were more than mere mortals; they were "heaven's anointed, the only truly liberated people on earth" (273).

Regardless of whether or not they are truly excused from ordinary rules of behavior, on the surface they seem to act as if they are. But Capote was wrong in thinking they follow no rules at all, and he learned just how wrong he was when he broke their rules and found himself an outcast. He betrayed confidences, spread rumors, gossiped incorrigibly, broke up marriages, was, in short, disloyal; and for this disloyalty he paid the price of losing his "guest membership in [their] celestial society" (274).

It is not hard to see that a mentality that defers to aristocratic power is very likely to hold the democratic process in contempt as well as all the dullness and pettiness and cowardice that presumably go with it. What is harder to understand is how a mind that can be so sharp and so alert when it is coldly observing the folly of the world can be so easily taken in by some of the world's greatest fools.

One has only to think of Ezra Pound and his fascist sympathies to get some idea of how madmen like Hitler and Mussolini can bewitch the gullible artist. The Canadian novelist Timothy Findley, in his highly original novel *Famous Last Words,* writes of the existence of an elite international cabal that flourished clandestinely during the second world war. The figure at the center of this curious blend of fact and fiction bears the name of Ezra Pound's persona Hugh Selwyn Mauberley, a poet who joins with many of the most celebrated figures of the day in a plot to set up a world state with the Duke and Duchess of Windsor as its ruling monarchs. Lieutenant Quinn, who narrates this story, finds Mauberley's body in the courtyard of an abandoned hotel high in the Italian Alps just as the war is ending. He also finds that the walls of room after room in the hotel have been covered with Mauberley's exhaustive history of this infamous cabal.

It is a provocative story, compelling and believable, and Findley is brilliant in the way he gives the plot and the people who hatch it the harrowing ring of truth. The members of the cabal plan to offer support to the Germans in exchange for German cooperation after the war. The way this cooperation is to be gained is by making a separate deal with General von Ribbentrop to overthrow Hitler and replace him with von Ribbentrop as more or less a figurehead. Meanwhile, the Windsors would be running the show. It is admittedly a bizarre plot, and in lesser hands would be nothing more than a highly imaginative diversion, but Findley is no hack, and what he reveals about the "delusions of grandeur" that can possess a mind as brilliant, as arrogant, and as tormented as Pound's justifies the fantasy of the rest of it (if, indeed, it really is a fantasy, for it sounds like something Mrs. Simpson might have fallen for). Certainly, Findley's fantasy is one way to try to penetrate the mind of a genius like Pound who let himself be duped into making treasonable, anti-Semitic, pro-fascist broadcasts during a war that had none of the ambiguities of the conflict in Vietnam.

Perhaps the most unsettling example of a brilliant mind at war with itself and susceptible to radical solutions is that of Franz Kafka, the last person one would expect to succumb to the lure of extreme ideologies. The side of him that understood the will to power better than anyone in this century is revealed in "In the Penal Colony." Although, as we have seen, there are graphic scenes in this story of diabolical torture, the story is not about torture but about power. An early reviewer, the only one to appreciate the genius of the story when it first appeared, pointed out that the officer who operates the machine is really amoral, that he is no torturer, not even a sadist, because he is more interested in the smooth functioning of the machine than in the suffering of the victim. It is a fine line, indeed, and one could argue that indifferent torture may even go beyond sadism to something indescribably more evil.

Nevertheless, the officer's preoccupation with the machine does highlight another dimension of the decadent vulnerability to the kind of political authority and detachment that the machine represents. This same reviewer comments on the officer's "boundless, slavish worship of the machine, which [the officer] calls justice and which in fact is power. Power without limits. To be able for once to exercise power without any constraints," muses the reviewer, who then compares this fantasy with adolescent sexual fantasies. "What stimulates them is not just sex," he points out, "but the absence of constraints. To be able to impose one's will, without any limits. This," he says, "is the dream that Kafka's story is about, and the obstacles in the way of perfect wish-fulfillment are part of it" (Pawel, 328).

However, much as he understood the danger and corruption of such a dream, Kafka also understood its deadly allure. In *The Nightmare of Reason,* Ernst Pawel explains it this way: Kafka was much too sane, he says, to fall for

the "marsh-gas mythologies of blood, sex, and race rising in dense cloud for-
mation from the ideological swamps of Europe." Even so, Pawel adds, he was
not immune to the influence of certain propagandists, "both Jews and Germans," whose ideas he was inclined to take much too seriously. Although he
didn't always agree with them, says Pawel, he "borrowed from their droppings
to indulge his self-disgust" (399–400).

The will to power begins, it would seem, in the desire to be free of all
constraints. Power without constraint: This mad illusion is the Achilles'
heel of decadence.

Conclusion

In the analysis of any state of mind or mode of behavior, one must always leave room for the inexplicable. Standing too near the object under scrutiny, looking too closely, focusing too sharply can cause the image to blur and dissolve, to fragment and disintegrate like a milkweed pod dropped upon a stone. What Isak Dinesen once said about literature could just as well be said about decadence: "You must take in whatever you can, and leave the rest outside, [for] it is not a bad thing in a tale that you understand only half of it" (*Seven,* 279).

I think decadence is all I have said it is—and more, for when it comes to a term as elusive as decadence, its whole really is greater than the sum of its parts. Therefore, to concentrate on its components item by item is to give each one a temporary magnification that distorts all proportion and makes it seem as if decadence is only that one thing, the thing that one happens to be analyzing at the moment. Then, suddenly, that one thing—be it hedonism, narcissism, irreverence, whatever—takes over and becomes the standard by which decadence is measured; and everybody who has ever lingered in a hot tub or kissed a mirror or uttered a smart-alecky remark is indiscriminately tossed on the dungheap and declared decadent.

This mistake occurs when the terms of the syllogism that defines decadence are reversed. For example, while it is true that there is a side to decadence that is irreverent, it is not true that anything that is irreverent is automatically decadent. And this goes for all the other elements of decadence. The world is full of naive people, most of whom are *not* decadent. But that does not alter the fact that, in addition to being naive, most decadents are also self-centered and masochistic and indifferent and most of the other things that together define the decadent personality. It is not until these ingredients coalesce that there is a context in which individual elements of decadence come into focus.

Each trait attributed to decadence must be viewed, therefore, within this decadent context and with the understanding that the sort of "compleat decadent" that bloomed in France and England at the end of the nineteenth century has not flowered in the twentieth. Even then the image of the decadent was something of a myth, but as such it was a fully realized image that artists like Mallarmé and Verlaine and Oscar Wilde and Aubrey Beardsley seemed to fit—in spite of the many scholarly attempts since then to prove that, whatever they were, they were *not* decadent.

In the meantime, the decadent personality (i.e., the image we retain of the myth) has splintered so that only shards appear here and there, and it is these that we measure against the prototype. The naiveté of Shaw and Lawrence is a decadent trait, the Pygmalionesque manipulation of others by Isak Dinesen and Truman Capote is a decadent trait, the masochism of Kafka and the sadism of Stephen King are decadent traits—all of these possessed by persons whose debt to decadence is clear but whose artistic center of gravity is obviously elsewhere.

It would be easy to retreat from describing the context in which ordinary behavior becomes decadent by arguing that to describe it is as difficult as describing a feeling of apprehension or a sense of foreboding that can overcome you at a moment when a sixth sense seems to tell you that you are in the presence of more than you can immediately see. But there is already something of a description in that evasion, for the presence of decadence is something that one really does sense, in a subtle but sure way, and it is possible to suggest some terms that one can associate with that sensation. Words like ripe and cloying, stifling and claustrophobic, cloistered and exotic are arrows that hit the target but miss the mark, for they leave out what is undeniably a sunnier side to decadence, most apparent in decadent wit. However, a metaphor like "hothouse" comes closer if only because it suggests something of an isolated, enclosed, and controlled environment in which the characters are confined as if under glass, in an artificially controlled culture.

The city of Venice works as an excellent metaphor to illustrate this hothouse analogy. Thomas Mann found it the ideal place to test Aschenbach's rigid self-discipline. There is something about the timelessness of Venice, something about its elegant seediness, its otherworldliness, its uniqueness that divorces the visitor from reality. It may be difficult to sit in the Piazza Navona in Rome and remember Peoria, but it is next to impossible to sit in the Piazza San Marco in Venice and remember very much of anything. This is the Venice of James's *The Aspern Papers,* a city in which it is entirely possible to imagine a reclusive mistress of a romantic poet still alive nearly a century later and still able to cast a spell over a dissembling young scholar who has himself lost track of time.

Strangers who wander through the labyrinthine back alleys of Venice, especially after dark, are apt to forget where they are—or even who they are. This is the case with the vacationing lovers in Ian McEwan's *The Comfort of Strangers,* the couple who find themselves the willing victims of the sort of skullduggery reminiscent of Iago's intrigues in *Othello*. It is also the same atmosphere Daphne du Maurier uses to such unnerving effect in her sinister short story "Don't Look Back" where the mood is darkened and the mystery intensified because the characters feel cut off and trapped. It is easy to become disoriented in a place that bears so little resemblance to the familiar world outside.

The hothouse atmosphere is also present to a suffocating degree at Bly, the country house in *The Turn of the Screw,* a place that stands as a symbol of the neurosis of the governess who has been repressed by a strict, religious up-bringing and driven to distraction by an overstimulated imagination. The life at Bly is so far removed from the outer world that it seems only natural that someone should begin to have hallucinations. To a lesser extent, the country house of Poynton serves a similar purpose, but in this case it is the furnishings that reinforce the effect, for when Mrs. Gareth has them transported to Ricks, a much smaller place, they take up so much space that there is scarcely enough room for her to get around.

Castalia, the mountain retreat in Hesse's *Magister Ludi* where Josef Knecht finds intellectual stimulation at the expense of involvement in the world out-side, is yet another example of the kind of isolation that breeds indifference and self-absorption. In this case, the knowledge acquired at Castalia is meant to serve no useful purpose; it is acquired merely for its own sake. Once Knecht leaves this rarified atmosphere, he is doomed to failure when he encounters the transactions and commitments that life in the real world requires for survival as well as fulfillment.

This sense of being isolated is present in decadent works from Dorian Gray's opium dens to the "Club de" of *Social Disease.* And in Tom Wolfe's *The Bonfire of the Vanities,* Sherman McCoy's life is spent shuttling from cell to cell in the prison of his privileged existence. In the opening scene, Sherman, feel-ing trapped in his Park Avenue apartment, schemes desperately to get out in order to call his mistress, Maria, without his wife's knowledge. When he does manage it, using the excuse of walking the dog even though it is raining, he gets trapped in a telephone booth with the dog's leash wrapped around his legs. Flustered, he dials his own number by mistake, and his wife answers. Later, when he is finally together with Maria in the tiny apartment she sublets from a friend, the claustrophobia mounts. At his job on Wall Street, Sherman is confined to a cubicle all day, unable to leave his desk without risking disap-proval and maybe even dismissal. He eats lunch at his desk, even has his shoes shined while he works. As he moves from cell to cell, Sherman feels like a condemned man.

Ironically, it is not long before he actually becomes a condemned man, forced to spend time in a holding cell while being brought up on charges of a hit-and-run accident involving a black teenager. The prison scenes are particu-larly harrowing, and not just because we know Sherman is innocent, but be-cause we are made to feel that one trap has merely been replaced with another.

Even the scene in which Sherman and Maria make a wrong turn on the way back from the airport and get lost in the Bronx is rendered in an atmosphere of entrapment. Locked in and lost, they drive in circles through deserted streets until they spot a ramp leading to the bridge to Manhattan. But there is a tire blocking the entrance to the ramp, and when they stop to remove it, two black teenagers move toward the car in what, to Sherman and Maria, is a distinctly threatening manner. At this point Sherman really does feel caught in a trap, and it is the fear and panic the situation creates that precipitates the plot.

Ever present throughout the novel is the sense of the larger cell in which Sherman dwells, the cell of his social class, those who move in narrow circles as if they really inhabited a small town. His is not the only class, however, to inhabit a cell. All the characters in this novel assume definition within the narrow confines of the space they inhabit, and it is interesting to note how much attention Wolfe gives to the details of that space, all the way from the real English fireplace in the office of Sherman's boss, installed to create the illusion of gracious country living in a glass and masonite room with an eight-foot ceiling, to the tacky waiting room complete with tilting plastic chairs in the office of Sherman's Irish lawyer.

This atmosphere of confinement that seems to permeate most literature with decadent overtones owes much to the maidens in locked towers of Gothic fiction and much more to the rooms and tombs of Edgar Allan Poe. Since then it has repeated itself in such places as Des Esseintes's suburban retreat, Dorian Gray's attic, Gregor Samsa's bedroom, Truman Capote's tree house, Jean-Baptiste Grenouille's mountain cave, Michael Chabon's sweltering Pittsburgh, and the back bedroom of Annie Wilkes's house in the Colorado mountains, the room in which Paul Sheldon is held prisoner and tortured. It suggests a latent fear, common to the decadent sensibility, of premature burial, not just in the physical sense of being buried alive but in the psychological sense of being smothered in the midst of life. Decadents have peculiarly immature fears and responses almost as if they were suspended in a state of arrested development that someone has referred to as "embalmed adolescence."

What is often inexplicable about decadence is its motivation, and an understanding of motivation is a necessary part of any analysis of behavior. Simply saying that a decadent has a fastidious nature or a taste for aesthetic thrills, that he feels estranged from society, that he has an irreverent wit and a preference for the artificial, that he can be cruel and irresponsible and outrageously self-centered is to identify, not to explain. Perhaps one way to explain what motivates decadents is to look at their heightened sensitivity to human folly. Decadent behavior arises from a desire to make society aware of its own foolishness by functioning as what the Germans call a *Zerrspiegel,* a mirror that distorts in such a way that the image being reflected sees itself in grotesque enlargement. Decadents may function as caricatures of society simply as a way of getting society to see itself as it really is. They may not hold out much hope of redemption, but their purpose is not to make matters worse. Decadents are not sociopaths.

It is not too much to say that decadents are, instead, the conscience of their age. After all, Oscar Wilde once said that conscience makes egotists of us all, and where you have overheated egos to begin with, conscience merely stokes the fire. Were there a decadent credo in this regard, it might come straight from the last page of Joyce's *Portrait of the Artist as a Young Man* where Stephen Dedalus pledges "to forge in the smithy of my soul the uncreated conscience of my race" (253). But the way the decadents go about it is not exactly what Stephen had in mind. They do things in excess partly to remind us of our own weaknesses, for decadence is ultimately a moral reminder, something of a *reductio ad absurdum* to show what happens when we go too far. Their sophistication ridicules our own sophistry. By mimicking our own hypocrisy, by forcing to the limit the things we think we can avoid by compromise, they make us see the evil in ourselves. There is a passage in *Against Nature* in which Des Esseintes exposes the hypocrisy of those who oppose abortion while at the same time doing everything possible to prevent conception. By defending infanticide as a reasonable alternative to abortion, he really does a good job of defending traditional Catholic morality in the same way Swift made a moral point by means of an immoral argument in "A Modest Proposal." Des Esseintes's point is that birth control is birth control, regardless of the method used, and his outrage at the specious reasoning of the hypocrites is an illustration of the way the decadent conscience, instead of being inoperative as is commonly thought, is actually highly acute.

Decadence pricks society's conscience by calling its bluff. What is hedonism but an exaggeration of society's tendency toward self-indulgence, toward conspicuous consumption, toward irresponsible self-gratification? And what is irresponsibility but a reminder of society's insensitivity and thoughtlessness, of its ruthless ambition that cares not whom it hurts? Irreverence can never erode a belief honestly arrived at and sincerely held, but it can make Swiss cheese out of borrowed beliefs and canned creeds. And in a world of cheap fakes, a world of dacron and polyester, of formica and astroturf, of laugh tracks and plastic "china," decadents, like Holly Golightly of *Breakfast at Tiffany's,* may be phonies, but they are "real phonies."

Decadent naiveté, like so many other decadent traits, is in many ways no more than a reflection of the gullibility of society at large. The world is full of people all too willing to fall for the casuists who, with a blend of sophistry and charisma, can offer them a system that serves their greed and satisfies their lusts. Systems that sanction immorality in the name of humanism, that bribe voters in the name of welfare, that blame "the thousand natural shocks that flesh is heir to" on medical malpractice, have a powerful attraction for those whose pastime is abusing their rights by pushing their luck.

For most people, decadence is a pejorative word, a way of labelling behavior that they think shows disrespect for their values. And perhaps this is as it should be, for decadence is always in opposition to the current standards of society and thus must always take its definition from those it offends. It is for this reason that some have thought it an elusive, a protean, an ultimately meaningless term. They want it to describe concrete behavior whereas what it describes is abstract behavior. Going against the grain takes different forms in different times. For example, Des Esseintes ridiculed anti-abortionists because he despised their mendacity, not because he favored abortion. Today, when values have shifted and abortion has become widely accepted, Huysmans might change his target, but not his tactics.

Decadence, then, is always relative to the time period it identifies. In *Decadent Societies,* Robert Adams is constantly reminding the reader that decadence is a comparative term as is, of course, any judgmental word, "and 'decadence,'" he says, "is nothing if not a judgmental word" (4). Decadent in comparison with what? is the critical question. My contention is that societies, regardless of how liberal they may seem, support a system of values (even non-values are values in the way that not getting an answer is an answer) by which contrary attitudes can be judged. If those contrary attitudes are intended more to outrage than enlighten, then decadence is present. It is the difference between the serious moralist who deplores the fearful legacy of the sexual revolution and the satirist who has nothing against sexual freedom but still finds things like the *Playboy* philosophy and other pious pronouncements about sex utterly absurd.

To maintain a perspective on decadence, it is necessary to keep in mind the root of the word decadence which is "a falling away from." One way to do this is to imagine the mainstream of society and then look at those who are standing back, stepping aside, moving over, in short, falling away from it. At its worst, decadence snubs its nose and does society's depravities one better, but at its best, decadence causes society to pull itself up short, draw in its breath, and maybe look twice at those practices that are inimical to its own best interests.

In her biography of Isak Dinesen, Judith Thurman tells the story of how deeply wounded Dinesen was by a Danish reviewer who viciously attacked *Seven Gothic Tales* as decadent and accused her of "coquetry and shallowness, caprice, mystification and false effects, snobbery, name dropping, and pastiche" (269). In the process of lamenting these ignorant distortions and coming to Dinesen's defense, Thurman has this to say: "Isak Dinesen was one of our most pure-hearted—not to say one of our greatest—immoralists" (270). What Thurman says of Dinesen could be said of all possessors of the true decadent spirit, that these soft-hearted cynics, these devout doubters, these altruistic egoists are, indeed, "pure-hearted immoralists."

Bibliography

Adams, Robert M. *Decadent Societies*. San Francisco: North Point, 1983.

———. *The Land and Literature of England*. New York: Norton, 1983.

Arnold, Matthew. "Stanzas from the Grande Chartreuse." In *The Norton Anthology of English Literature*. Edited by M. H. Abrams et al. 5th ed. 2 vols., 2: 1384–1390. New York: Norton, 1986.

Auster, Paul. *City of Glass*. New York: Penguin, 1987.

———. *Ghosts*. New York: Penguin, 1987.

Beardsley, Aubrey and John Glassco. *Under the Hill*. New York: Grove, 1959.

Beckson, Karl, ed. *Aesthetes and Decadents of the 1890s*. New York: Vintage Books, 1966.

Beerbohm, Max. "From '1880' in *The Yellow Book*." In *The Aesthetes: A Sourcebook*. Edited by Ian Small, 200–202. London: Routledge, 1979.

Bjørnvig, Thorkild. *The Pact: My Friendship with Isak Dinesen*. Translated by Ingvar Schousboe and William Jay Smith. Baton Rouge: Louisiana State UP, 1983.

Buchen, Irving. *The Perverse Imagination*. New York: New York UP, 1970.

Burgess, Anthony. Review of *Bernard Shaw 1856–1898: The Search for Love* by Michael Holroyd. *Atlantic* (Oct. 1988): 90–95.

Capote, Truman. *Answered Prayers*. New York: Random House, 1987.

———. *Breakfast at Tiffany's. Three by Truman Capote*. New York: Random, 1985: 135–184.

———. *Conversations*. Jackson: UP of Mississippi, 1987.

———. *The Dogs Bark: Public People & Private Places*. New York: NAL, 1977.

Chabon, Michael. *The Mysteries of Pittsburgh*. New York: Morrow, 1988.

Charlesworth, Barbara. *Dark Passages: The Decadent Consciousness in Victorian Literature*. Madison: U of Wisconsin P, 1965.

Clarke, Gerald. *Capote: A Biography*. New York: Simon and Schuster, 1988.

de Vries, Peter. *Slouching towards Kalamazoo*. Boston: Little, Brown, 1983.

Dijkstra, Bram. *Idols of Perversity: Fantasies of Feminine Evil in Fin-de-Siècle Culture*. New York: Oxford UP, 1986.

Dinesen, Isak. *Anecdotes of Destiny*. New York: Random House, 1958.

_____. "The Devil's Opponent." Unpublished story, 1904.

_____. *Ehrengard*. New York: Random House, 1963.

_____. *Last Tales*. New York: Random House, 1957.

_____. *Seven Gothic Tales*. New York: Random House, 1934.

Dostoyevsky, Feodor. *Notes from Underground. Short Novels of the Masters*. Edited by Charles Neider. New York: Holt, 1966.

Dowling, Linda C. *Aestheticism and Decadence: A Selective Annotated Bibliography*. New York: Garland, 1977.

du Maurier, Daphne. *The House on the Strand*. New York: Avon, 1970.

du Maurier, George. *Trilby*. New York: Harper, 1894.

Ellmann, Richard. *Oscar Wilde*. New York: Knopf, 1988.

Findley, Timothy. *Famous Last Words*. New York: Laurel, 1983.

Finney, Jack. *Time and Again*. New York: Simon and Schuster, 1970.

Firbank, Ronald. *The Flower Beneath the Foot. Two Novels*. New York: New Directions, 1962.

Fitzgerald, F. Scott. *The Beautiful and the Damned*. New York: Scribner's, 1922.

_____. *The Great Gatsby*. Scribner's, 1925.

_____. *The Rich Boy. Forms of the Novella*. Edited by David H. Richter. New York: Knopf, 1981.

Gide, André. *The Immoralist*. Translated by Richard Howard. New York: Vintage Books, 1970.

Gilman, Richard. *Decadence: The Strange Life of an Epithet*. New York: Farrar, 1979.

Goldfarb, Russell. "Late Victorian Decadence." *Journal of Aesthetics and Art Criticism* 20 (1962): 369–373.

Golding, William. *Pincher Martin*. New York: Capricorn, 1956.

Gorer, Geoffrey. *The Life and Ideas of the Marquis de Sade*. New York: Norton, 1963.

Greene, Graham. *A Burnt-Out Case*. New York: Viking, 1961.

_____. *Doctor Fischer of Geneva or the Bomb Party*. New York: Simon and Schuster, 1980.

_____. *The Heart of the Matter*. New York: Viking, 1948.

_____. *Monsignor Quixote*. New York: Simon and Schuster, 1982.

_____. *The Power and the Glory*. New York: Viking, 1946.

_____. *Travels with My Aunt*. New York: Viking, 1970.

Hannah, Donald. *Isak Dinesen & Karen Blixen: The Mask and the Reality*. London: Putnam, 1971.

Hauser, Arnold. *The Social History of Art*. Vol. 2. New York: Knopf, 1951.

Hesse, Hermann. *Demian*. New York: Bantam, 1966.

_____. *Magister Ludi: The Glass Bead Game*. New York: Bantam, 1970.

Huxley, Aldous. *Crome Yellow*. New York: Harper, 1922.

_____. *Time Must Have a Stop*. New York: Harper, 1965.

Huysmans, J.-K. *Against Nature*. Translated by Robert Baldick. New York: Penguin, 1959.

Isherwood, Christopher. "Sally Bowles." *Good-bye to Berlin*. New York: Random House, 1939.

Jackson, Holbrook. *The Eighteen Nineties*. New York: Capricorn, 1966.

James, Henry. *The Art of the Novel*. New York: Scribner's, 1937.

_____. *The Spoils of Poynton*. New York: Penguin, 1963.

_____. *The Turn of the Screw* and *Daisy Miller*. New York: Dell, 1954.

————. *Washington Square*. New York: Modern Library, 1950.

Joad, Cyril E.M. *Decadence: A Philosophical Inquiry*. New York: Philosophical Library, 1949.

Johanneson, Eric O. *The World of Isak Dinesen*. Seattle: U of Washington P, 1961.

Joyce, James. *Portrait of the Artist as a Young Man*. Edited by Chester G. Anderson. New York: Viking, 1968.

Jullian, Philippe. *Dreamers of Decadence*. New York: Praeger, 1971.

Kafka, Franz. *The Castle*. New York: Knopf, 1961.

————. "In the Penal Colony." In *Selected Short Stories*. New York: Modern Library, 1952.

————. "The Metamorphosis." In *Selected Short Stories*. New York: Modern Library, 1952.

————. *The Trial*. New York: Modern Library, 1937.

Kanfer, Stefan. Review of *Bernard Shaw 1856–1898: The Search for Love* by Michael Holroyd. *Time* (6 June 1988): 87.

Kerouac, Jack. *On the Road*. New York: Viking, 1955.

King, Stephen. *Misery*. New York: Viking, 1987.

Laing, R.D. *The Politics of Experience*. New York: Pantheon, 1967.

Langbaum, Robert. *The Gayety of Vision*. New York: Random House, 1965.

Lodge, David. *Changing Places*. Bath, England: Chivers, 1986.

————. *Small World*. New York: Penguin, 1985.

————. *Souls and Bodies. (How Far Can You Go?)* New York: Penguin, 1981.

Mann, Thomas. *Death in Venice. Short Novels of the Masters*. Edited by Charles Neider. New York: Holt, 1966.

————. *The Magic Mountain*. Translated by H.T. Lowe-Porter. New York: Vintage Books, 1969.

————. "Mario and the Magician." In *Classic Short Fiction*. Edited by James K. Bowen and Richard VanDerBeets, 14–48. New York: Bobbs-Merrill, 1972.

Maugham, W. Somerset. *The Moon and Sixpence*. New York: Doran, 1919.

————. "The Outstation." In *Short Story Masterpieces*. Edited by Robert Penn Warren and Albert Erskine, 289–322. New York: Dell, 1958.

————. *The Razor's Edge*. Philadelphia: Triangle, 1946.

McEwan, Ian. *The Comfort of Strangers*. New York: Washington Square, 1981.

McInerney, Jay. *Bright Lights, Big City*. New York: Vintage Books, 1984.

————. *Ransom*. New York: Vintage Books, 1985.

Nabokov, Vladimir. *Lolita*. New York: Putnam, 1958.

O'Connor, Flannery. "Good Country People." In *Reading and Writing about Short Fiction*. Edited by Edward Proffitt, 416–433. New York: Harcourt, 1988.

Pater, Walter. *Appreciations*. London: Macmillan, 1910.

————. *Marius, the Epicurean. The Aesthetes*. Edited by Ian Small, 136–148. London: Routledge, 1979.

————. *The Renaissance*. London: Macmillan, 1910.

Pawel, Ernst. *The Nightmare of Reason: A Life of Franz Kafka*. New York: Farrar, 1984.

Peters, Robert L. "Toward an 'Un-Definition' of Decadent." *Journal of Aesthetics and Art Criticism* 18 (1959): 258–264.

Pierrot, Jean. *The Decadent Imagination 1800–1900*. Translated by Derek Coltman. Chicago: U of Chicago P, 1981.

Praz, Mario. *The Romantic Agony.* New York: Oxford UP, 1970.

Rand, Ayn. *The Fountainhead.* New York: Bobbs-Merrill, 1943.

Redman, Alvin. *The Wit and Humor of Oscar Wilde.* New York: Dover, 1959.

Reed, John R. *Decadent Style.* Athens: Ohio UP, 1985.

Rudnick, Paul. *Social Disease.* New York: Knopf, 1986.

Ryals, Clyde de L. "Towards a Definition of *Decadent* as applied to British Literature in the Nineteenth Century." *Journal of Aesthetics and Art Criticism* 17 (1958): 85–92.

Salinger, J.D. *The Catcher in the Rye.* New York: Signet, 1953.

Seymour-Smith, Martin. *Who's Who in Twentieth Century Literature.* New York: McGraw Hill, 1977.

Shaw, George Bernard. *Pygmalion.* Baltimore: Penguin, 1951.

Skow, John. Review of *Capote* by Gerald Clarke. *Time* (30 May 1988): 60.

Small, Ian, ed. *The Aesthetes.* London: Routledge, 1979.

Sontag, Susan. "Notes on Camp." *Against Interpretation.* New York: Farrar, 1966.

Süskind, Patrick. *Perfume.* Translated by John E. Woods. New York: Pocket Books, 1987.

Symons, Arthur. "The Decadent Movement in Literature." In *Aesthetes and Decadents of the 1890s.* Edited by Karl Beckson, 134–151. New York: Vintage Books, 1966.

Thompson, Hunter S. *Fear and Loathing in Las Vegas.* New York: Warner, 1983.

_____. "The Kentucky Derby is Decadent and Depraved." In *The New Journalism.* Edited by Tom Wolfe and E.W. Johnson, 172–187. New York: Harper, 1973.

Thornton, R.K.R. *The Decadent Dilemma.* London: Edward Arnold, 1983.

Thurman, Judith. *Isak Dinesen: The Life of a Storyteller.* New York: St. Martin's, 1982.

Waugh, Evelyn. *Brideshead Revisited.* New York: Dell, 1960.

_____. *Decline and Fall.* New York: Grosset, n.d.

Wilde, Oscar. "The Decay of Lying." *The Portable Oscar Wilde.* Edited by Richard Aldington. New York: Penguin, 1946.

_____. *The Picture of Dorian Gray. The Portable Oscar Wilde.* Edited by Richard Aldington, 138–391. New York: Penguin, 1946.

Williams, Tennessee. *A Streetcar Named Desire.* New York: Signet, 1951.

Wivel, Ole. *Romance for Valdhorn.* Copenhagen: Gyldendal, 1972.

Wolfe, Tom. *The Bonfire of the Vanities.* New York: Farrar, 1987.

_____. *From Bauhaus to Our House.* New York: Farrar, 1981.

_____. *The Painted Word.* New York: Farrar, 1975.

_____. *The Purple Decades.* New York: Farrar, 1982.

_____. *Radical Chic & Mau-Mauing the Flak Catchers.* New York: Farrar, 1970.

Index

About the Author

THOMAS REED WHISSEN, Professor of English at Wright State University, is the author of *A Way with Words, Components of Composition, Isak Dinesen's Aesthetics,* and journal articles and has contributed chapters on topics in literature and composition.